The Road No One One

Traveled

Raymond Kiddy

ISBN: 978-1-968985-45-5

Published by

Global Ink Publishing Inc.
www.globalinkpublishinginc.com

Printed in the United States of America

Dedication

This book is dedicated to my wife, Lori (Richmond) Kiddy

My children Ross, Garrett, and Gabe

My daughters-in-law Erin, Kelsey, and Andriana

My grandchildren

My sister, Catherine, and her husband, Tim Miller

In-laws, Bill and Judy Richmond

In memory of my parents, Faye and Maxine Kiddy

All of the players, coaches, mentors, and friends I have been associated with over the years.

Above all, blessings from God.

Acknowledgement

I had always wanted to be a coach from the age of ten. Back then, I didn't know what it would take to be a coach. Actually, I didn't know how many people in my life it would take to support a coach for forty-two years until my career was over. The vast number of people who influence your life during your career are underappreciated. I would like to thank all of the players, coaches, and mentors who have supported me.

I am sure my memory is good, not great! To those who find a story that involved you, and my recollection is different than yours, please forgive me. The content included is, to the best of my recollection.

I would like to thank all of my colleagues, friends, and administrators who shared the dream of educating our youth at thirteen different schools and colleges.

Also, I would like to thank the Christian Brothers of Bishop Walsh School, who had confidence in me and gave me my first coaching responsibilities.

I would also like to thank Vince Celtnieks, Jay Hegeman, and Rick Zimmerman, who allowed this coach to be their assistant during the growing process.

Special thanks to my wife, Lori, who proofread my master's thesis, doctoral dissertation, and my first book.

Also, thanks to Jeanne Boardman, my editor, and Andy Zhao, illustrator. This book would not be possible without the support of Global Ink Publishing Inc. and Bob Collins at Global, who provided me with guidance and pep talks through the entire process as my personal publishing manager.

My life has always been about faith, family, and work.

-Ray Kiddy

Table of Contents

Foreword i

Introduction: A Season to Forget! iv

Chapter 1: Take Your Mark-Get Set! 19

Chapter 2: College Days 27

Chapter 3: Bishop Walsh Opens the Door 32

Chapter 4: The Key to Success is Organization! 35

Chapter 5: Anxiety Gains a Life of Its Own 40

Chapter 6: Keep Your Head Up 48

Chapter 7: What is Up Around the Bend? 55

Chapter 8: Promise 67

Chapter 9: Change 73

Chapter 10: Finale One 76

Chapter 11: Indiana University of Pennsylvania 82

Chapter 12: Two Years-Three College Teams 90

Chapter 13: Gun Shy 101

Chapter 14: Another Opportunity 128

Chapter 15: Well, Why Would You Stay? 137

Chapter 16: Keep Your Feet Moving 147

Chapter 17: Allegany Again 160

Chapter 18: Steps to Becoming an Indian 169

Chapter 19: Consolidated 178

Chapter 20: Rules and Regulations 193

Chapter 21: Caught the Bug Again 197

Chapter 22: Worst Assistant Coach Ever 209

Chapter 23: A Labor of Love 216

Chapter 24: Recovery 255

Chapter 25: The Union 263

Chapter 26: Finale Two 267

Author's Note 274

Appendix 275

Foreword

Ray and I broke in together at Bishop Walsh High School in 1979. We were both twenty-two year old teachers. He really has not changed. Ray has always been friendly and kind. When I organized a field trip in the fall of our first year, Ray was eager to chaperone. We went to Harper's Ferry and Antietam and just like now, Ray was great company and helpful.

Ray enjoys noting the fact that he is a Presbyterian principal of a Catholic school. But I have never met anyone who better exemplifies Judeo-Christian values than Ray. Remember the Gospel from Holy Thursday when Jesus washed the feet of the disciples as a sign of service? I have never worked with anyone more interested in pitching in to help than Ray. Whether it's physical labor, moral support, or just a friendly talk, Ray is there using his leadership position as one of service to others. When Ray an I broadcast soccer games together, Ray puts up the WCBC banner, helps carry equipment and offers me French fries every broadcast. I could never ask for a better partner who is fun and conscientious. Ray also developed a zany Goal!!!!! call. The fans really enjoyed it.

I think another image that suits Ray is the poem called Footprints in the Sand. In this poem a man dreams that there are two sets of footprints on the beach, signifying that Jesus walked alongside him. However, during sad and difficult times, there was only one set of footprints and the man asked Jesus why he left him alone during tough times? Jesus answered that during those difficult periods Jesus was carrying the man to safety. Well, Ray has done that for Bishop Walsh. Two years ago, our future was in peril as the Archdiocese of Baltimore told us they could no longer carry a school in such debt. Ray picked up our entire community and enrollment increased tremendously. Our favorite Presbyterian made sure we were no longer on the chopping block. Ray carried us through that existential crisis.

So how did Ray revitalize our school and its enrollment? He didn't overturn the money changers tables in the temple as Jesus did; I think it was closer to Jesus raising Lazarus. We are in the poorest of Maryland's twenty-three counties with a declining population for decades. Ray didn't stabilize enrollment; he increased it by dozens of new students. And it wasn't just boys' basketball, which certainly was a bold decision. Ray awakened a dormant girl's athletic program with new students playing softball, basketball, volleyball, and soccer. Winning seasons returned. Ray would be the first to tell you he had plenty of help along the way; there were many disciples. But it all starts with organization, leadership, and without Ray I don't think we would have our current Pre-K-12 school here on Haystack Mountain.

For teachers and students, Ray welcomed everyone. He was patient with all of us. He was the longest serving lay principal in school history up to 2025. What a joy it has been to look forward to coming to work every day and just being able to do our job. Ray has been there to advise us, help us and support us. He trusts his people. Not every boss is like that. I think we've been spoiled.

Ray was our principal four years and he had hired over half of the faculty. Almost the entire elementary faculty has changed and there have been many changes in middle school and high school. Ray has hired good people. The proof is in what we have accomplished during Ray's three months of COVID with distance learning. Ray trusted us to do our jobs and we came through for students.

Ray likes to joke that he has told his wife Lori, that when he passes from this life, he wants her to say, "He was here a minute ago." Ray, as a colleague for over 40 years, a broadcast partner, an employee, and fervent support of Bishop Walsh, I thank you! I know you will enjoy the book!

Jim Zamagias

Forty-five year servant at Bishop Walsh School as history and political science teacher, Athletic Director, and Dean of Academics. WCBC radio sports team member for over 30 years.

Introduction: A Season to Forget!

"Have you hugged your kid today?"

-Morgan Wooten

Our children are fragile. We need to remind ourselves to build up our children each and every day. Our education system does more to bring children down than build them up.

A new situation needs to be observed-no action needed now.

If you are not excited about a new season, something is wrong.

Confidence is needed in all parts of life.

When life is going well, beware, the road of life has curious turns.

Don't be afraid to show your emotions.

You pass through life, it hits you, it loves your and you need to be there for others.

I had been coaching soccer for thirty-nine fall seasons. What happened during that thirty-nineth booter season was unexplainable, ungodly, and was met head on by a school soccer family that was unmatched by any 3-12 team ever. Speaking at the end of the season girls' soccer banquet in November 2017, I said "There is not one player, coach, or parent in this room that was not affected or changed by the events of the past three months."

The 2017 Bishop Walsh girls' soccer team lost eleven regular season games, one mother, a brother, a grandmother and two playoff games. As their head coach, I saw this team lose confidence, team play, faith in their faith, and one player to a torn ACL. I also saw them gain mental strength, social togetherness, and a blank stare that reminded me of the show "The Walking Dead."

I started coaching soccer at Bishop Walsh High School during the 1978 fall boys' soccer season. I was hired to coach the very first varsity boys' soccer team ever at the school during my senior year of college. Prior to my coaching beginning I played soccer at Valley High School in Lonaconing and junior college soccer at Allegany Community College in Cumberland, Maryland. I had earned several honors while playing the game at the two schools. But none of those honors matched the privilege of coaching those girls of the Bishop Walsh girls' soccer team of 2017.

My thirty-nine years of coaching soccer stretched from high school to NCAA Division II. This experience included one travel team, seven high schools, seven colleges, and one professional team affiliate. I would become bored with a place and moved on when we had some success. The challenge left and so did I.

My return to Bishop Walsh after departing back in 1985 was to return as the Athletic Director (AD) and to head up the girls' soccer program. Yes, I named myself head girls' soccer coach. I was the AD and soon to become the Head Master of Bishop Walsh School. The one year I was AD and became the girls coach was following a season when the girls had already suffered a season when their female head coach had an affair with one of the players on the 2016 team.

Donnie Amann became my assistant coach for the girls' team. Donnie coached several stints as a head and assistant soccer coach at the high school level. He also was an assistant at Potomac State College with their women's team for ten years. Donnie was a dependable assistant coach and he and I were friends during our high school years at different schools. Donnie grew up in Westernport, Maryland just six miles down the "crick" from Lonaconing, Maryland.

Coach Amann was a great practice coach but could be a nightmare on game day. He once yelled twenty seconds into a game that a particular girl was "killing the team." Really Donnie? Twenty seconds into the game. A coach could only have time to sit down after the "Star-Spangled Banner" had concluded in twenty seconds. Did she miss a trap, leave her marking, or just plain melt into the turf after your comment?

Donnie played the game in high school and had experience with some adult league play later in life. He knew the game and was very knowledgeable of all positions. I relied on and needed Donnie for what was about to come down on the Bishop Walsh girls' varsity soccer team during the fall of 2017.

Practice? Did You Say Practice?

We began practice on August 1, 2017. Nineteen players strong and the excitement of the new season was upon us. This was the first season for Donnie and I with this team. The girls were bitter about the past chatter of the 2016 and were anxious to put it behind them. The unfolding of information of a female coach in a relationship with their fellow teammate rocked the school community and the Archdiocese of Baltimore. Not what a Catholic education organization needed after the unveiling of decades of abuse by male leaders world-wide in the Catholic church.

We had to move on. That story was unfortunate yet it could not come close to what was about to happen over the next three months to nineteen young soccer players. Maybe that scandal was preparing us for what was about to come. They say God works in mysterious ways. Yes, he/she had mysterious things in the works for us.

Practice started with the usual Cooper Test. A twelve-minute run on the 400-meter track. You measure the distance covered by each athlete and the last lap in eights for a twelve-minute run. As predicted, we were out of shape measured by the results. We had twenty-one days to improve our conditioning, skill level and to mesh as a team.

The pressure was fun for our coaching duo! We had a new team that would be a challenge. That is what wets the whistle of any coach at the beginning of each season. The pieces come together for each coach every season. Sometimes the pieces fit early and sometimes way too late to salvage a season. This is why coaches refer to the playoffs at the end of the season as the second season or the final chapter. You are only heading in one direction at the end of a season. During 2017, the playoffs at the end of season were a sign of relief from the tragedies that had just occurred the past three months.

The preseason scrimmage was in Rockwood out of Pennsylvania with a steady girls' program that was always a very physical team. I always considered PA to have great youth programs. They appear to have it right from player registration, age grouping, youth sports development, scheduling, coaching training, and just plain efficiency. We finished the August 10th morning with a 3-1 loss. Still, I thought we saw promise and were competitive.

We had 19 players in the fall of 2017 and only one senior. Only having one senior can give you an inkling about the prospect of a solid season. Nevertheless, I thought our twelve juniors were a good athletic class. Our future seemed bright.

We opened with a 2-1 victory over Frankfort High School. We won the game in overtime. The girls tied Frankfort in the 2016 season. We then hosted Keyser High School and won 5-0. Again, a team we tied last year. We were starting to roll and defeated Petersburg 7-0. Petersburg was a poor skilled squad with few players and no self-confidence. Confidence is the key to success in all parts of life and was about to depart the 2017 Bishop Walsh girls' soccer team.

We had four games during the month of August 2017 before the bottom fell out of the season. Death occurred and was the worst two months of my life as a person and soccer coach. It changed me forever.

We held practice on Friday September 1 before giving the girls two days off. We were three 3-0 and feeling pretty good about ourselves. Always a heavy anchor to carry when you are not a consistently winning program. We had a winners practice that day. A winners practice in my coaching career consisted of discussing the past win, good or bad, and involved drills that are fun, a forty-five minute scrimmage! Most important for players, no conditioning during the winners' practice.

Labor Day

Practice ended that day and Donnie and I had gathered all the equipment with the help of the players. Erin Langan, our junior forward was dragging up the rear of girls walking the 100 yards to our locker room. It was obvious she wanted to talk to the coaches. "How are you Erin"? "Fine, but I do not think I will be at practice Monday (Labor Day)." We had a game Tuesday so we planned a walk through on Monday evening. Erin didn't like to miss practice. This statement from Erin caught me off guard. She said her mother was saying some strange things to her and her dad. They were both concerned and her dad (Steve), was taking Debbie Langan, Erin's Mom to Ruby Memorial Hospital in Morgantown, WV for a checkup. Erin said if they had to admit her mom, they could have a busy weekend and she would not make the next practice. I said "OK," but thought nothing of it other than concern for a parent of a player. However, I thought everything would be ok. I asked Erin to keep me posted on her mom and hopefully "See you Monday."

On Tuesday morning the school was buzzing as usual about exploits over the holiday weekend. However, It was different for the girls' soccer team. Word had spread that Erin Langan's mom had a brain tumor (Gliobastoma Multiforme). My first thoughts when I heard the news was that I need to see Erin but that was not possible because as I suspected, she was not at school that day. I switched my thoughts to the girls on the team, trying to seek them out during the school day before practice. All of the girls were down and I reminded them that we at Bishop Walsh are a praying institution and not only because she was Erin's mom. Debi Langan was a key leader in our school, heading many school fundraising activities. She helped keep BW afloat financially. All private Catholic schools have a handful of people who make a school a safe house for the school community and Debi was one of those special people.

She had charisma and a beautiful smile. She was a great parent. She was a pale skin, beautiful woman who wore bright red lipstick to offset her facial features. Debi's husband, Steve, was an engineer and he and Debi ran a successful construction business. Steve has a son Ryan, and one daughter Erin. This was a family that had everything. They had worked hard in their lives to get to this point, and now the rug was being ripped out from under them.

Debi had several major surgeries while in Morgantown at J.W Ruby Memorial. J.W. Ruby Memorial is a great hospital for the state of West

Virginia. It is an 880-bed tertiary care center. Ruby Memorial also serves as an academic medical center of the West Virginia University School of Medicine.

The surgeries involved removing the tumor while still leaving as much of Debi's brain for her to function. She was wheel chair bound and speech was difficult, following the multiple surgeries.

Erin was hit or miss for the next couple of games. Erin's moms' health deteriorated and as expected, as a team, we struggled big time, losing to cross town rivals Allegany and Fort Hill. Erin was missing practice now and then but did her best to continue to still be part of the team. As a coaching staff, we tried to keep the players motivated and supportive, bringing the juice needed to keep everyone in good spirits. The juice is energy to keep everyone supportive of each other to prove to the soul that everything will be ok.

Our next game was with the Allegany Campers at Greenway Avenue Stadium. They had already beat us 6-0 in a game without Erin. Donnie and I decided to play a more defensive minded game, known as "parking the bus" in soccer, against the Campers. It was also going to be a special afternoon. Erin's mom was released from the hospital and Steve was going to bring Debi to the game.

We all knew the prognosis for Debi and we were thinking this could be the last time she will see Erin play ever! We played defensively, keeping the ball out of the defensive end and trying to get a break away on a foul against Allegany. With ten minutes to go, their leading scorer put one in the net for a 1-0 lead and that is how the game ended. Still, I was so proud of our team having battled one of the top teams in the area to a tight game. I spoke to the team and let them know they had accomplished their mission today. Now lets' go into the stands and visit with Erin's mom.

I led the team up the ramp to see Debi. I shook Steve's hand and hugged Debi, telling her how proud we all were of her and the battle she is fighting. I let Debi know our battle in the field today was for her. We all cried as each player hugged Debi. We then went home to lick our wounds after the loss. But more importantly to think about the road of life and its curious turns.

Death Strikes

Early morning, the next day, I was sitting in my office following morning announcements. I was looking out my office window as the Principal of BW and I saw Erin giving her mom a long hug outside Steve's car. I was trying to think about what was going through both of their minds. Will we see each other again? Why is this happening? Will this situation get better? Can there be a miracle? They ended the long embrace and Erin entered the school building in tears. Steve drove Debi back to Ruby Memorial, where she died just two days later.

The funeral was on a Friday. I planned for the entire high school student body to attend the funeral if they wished. Every high school student had permission from their parent/guardian to attend the funeral.

This was such a tribute to Debi and the meaning of her work at Bishop Walsh School.

Erin, only a junior that fall, gave the eulogy for her mother. I do not know how Erin, who had been through so much in the past month, had the courage and poise to deliver a moving good bye that described the life of her mother.

Where do we go from here as the Bishop Walsh Girl's Team? The next practices were different without Erin's presence and leadership as one of our top players. Debi's time was short. We had prayed it would be longer than just the two days God had planned. Donnie and I knew this was not going to be easy but we had to refocus the team on the remainder of the season. The first practice following the weekend after the funeral was difficult. Still, it was good to get outside on the pitch, blow off the dust, and to think about something other than what had just occurred to our teammates' family. Our next game would be Petersburg, a team we could beat and celebrate something for a change. When it rains it pours, and it did, cancelling the next day's game with Petersburg.

We practiced the following day, September 28, 2017. It was a good practice and the next day, we hosted the Northern Huskies of Garrett County, Maryland for our soccer homecoming. Our problems in life followed us to the field. When people say, "It is just a game," as fans, they are right. But to those who have trained to prepare for the game, when training can last for several months, years, or entire career as a coach, college player, or a professional athlete, that game becomes your life! It was my life and my family's life. All of us involved are living it everyday of our lives. You can try not to bring your life's work home but it is difficult. A "For sale" sign can just appear in your yard following a loss! That doesn't happen in most homes unless the police are involved!

Back to that 2017 soccer homecoming game with the Northern Huskies team was a game we could win and needed to win for everyone in the BW community. The game was a hard-fought battle. We lost on a corner kick because of miscommunication between one back and our goalkeeper. You work on communication constantly at practice to the point that everyone is on the same page. Where were our heads on this play? This was, for me, the signal that we were playing uptight and probably would continue unless we could refocus from our woes. The Northern Huskies beat us that Homecoming Day 1-0. We were now 3-6 into the season and the month of September was over. Maybe October would be a better month for us?

The next week we practiced Monday and Tuesday to prepare for Fort Hill, another city rival. Tuesday following practiced we talked about transportation, arrival time and pre-game preparation. Nevertheless, I was not prepared for what was next to come into the saga that continued for Bishop Walsh soccer team of 2017.

Death Strikes Again

After we departed the practice field, Donnie and I sat outside the locker room waiting for all the girls to leave. This was our ritual. We would lock up equipment and the locker room for the evening. One of our players, who lived close to the school, walked home and found her 9th grade brother dead in the basement of their house. The police determined he died of a gunshot wound. I can't imagine finding anyone dead in your home. But definitely not by a gunshot wound. I happened to be driving by her home when I saw the police and a rescue squad arrive. I immediately pulled into a neighbor's driveway across the street. The neighbor told me what had happened. I got into my car and began crying.

That night, I had many phone calls from players and parents letting me know what they had heard. Our player's brother was not a student at Bishop Walsh. I called the administration of Allegany High School, where he had been attending. After interviewing the young man's friends, they all said he seemed fine during the school day and even set up his instrument station to attend a late evening band rehearsal and departed for home. He had been a part of an award-winning band of Allegany High School. The police investigation ruled his death as accidental.

My thoughts were these: No family should have to go through the loss of a mother or a brother/sibling period. They say God only gives you as much as you can handle when it comes to the good, the bad, the ugly. I was not sure how much more 19 girls could handle as a team. I knew it will take all we had to pull together, stick together and just plain comfort each other. Some teams face tragedy during their season, but in over 39 years of coaching, I had never been associated with a team that had their life and the way they looked at life change so drastically within a three-month period.

Donnie and I talked at length about how to handle the remainder of the season. We decided to cancel our next games with Fort Hill and Mountain Ridge. That would give us a week to recover, support the death of the brother of our teammate, and attend a memorial service. We actually gathered for practiced three times that week to talk, comfort each other, and kick around the ball to see if we even wanted to complete the season with 13 days remaining.

At practice, it was obvious to Donnie and I that the girls loved playing the game. Legendary Mount Savage Coach, George Bishields, once told me he only enjoyed practice. "I wish we never played the games," said George. He won more soccer games than anyone in Western Maryland. When you are at practice you are free of pressure, other than what you put on yourself. As a coach you are teaching and loving the game.

Is This Real Life?

The next week we played two games and then found out a grandmother of one of players had died. We went to the funeral home again to support a teammate. As you read this, you have to think this book must be fiction. This is real life and 2017 Bishop Walsh girls' soccer team lived and survived!

We finished the season with a trip to the Private School State Tournament in Hagerstown, Maryland. This involved two days in a hotel, attending Mass, good competition and a chance to be together. We lost both days. We lost to St. Maria Goretti 0-3 and to St. Marys' Riken 2-3.

St. Marys' Riken won the tournament and I was proud of our ladies fight that weekend. They were no longer girls but young ladies, who had withstood the test of life.

We completed the season with a record of 3-12. I can never forget the leadership that our only senior, Kyara Bible provided. Kyara Bible and Erin Langan led us in goals and assists with 16 and 19 points respectively. I also can never forget Donnie Amann who I could not have gotten through the 2017 season without. Sometimes we didn't say anything, we just sat there with more questions than answers.

Rosie Duncan was named First Team All-Area, Shianne Cromwell Second Team, and Kyara Bible Honorable Mention. Rosie Duncan was named All AMAC First Team, Kyara Bible Second Team, and Erin Langan Honorable Mention. Named to the All-City Team was Rosie Duncan and Shianne Cromwell. All Bi-State was Jordan Marini, Erin Langan and Kyara Bible.

At the end of the season banquet I noted that our team had lost eight games by one or two goals. The five teams that finished in the area above us beat us by a total of 7 goals. I said we had made great progress during August and the first part of September. But at that point, we just supported and hugged each other. I ended with this: "Everyone in this room has been changed by the past three months. No one is the same person in this room today, that you were in August 2017. We cried, we laughed, we won, we lost, but most importantly we loved each other as God has taught us. Always remember that God is always with us."

That winter our teammate, Kyara Bible, our only senior, joined an elite club in girls' basketball by scoring 1,000 points during her career at Bishop Walsh School. Kyara Bible survived the 2017 girls' soccer season at Bishop Walsh. She survived, learned and moved on. This was great for us to witness and learn from. It may have just happened yesterday. You pass through life, it hits you, it loves you and you need to be there for others! Thanks Kyara!

I started this book with the 2017 season because that is when I decided I should write my coaching memoir. I started writing my memoir in January of 2023 and it has taken me two and half years to complete. The chapters that follow are in chronological order. Read on!

Make sure your children know they are loved!

Chapter 1: Take Your Mark-Get Set!

"Our life is frittered away by detail, Simplify, Simplify."

-Henry David Thoreau

We all have fond memories of our youth. Cherish, rehash, and share those memories. It keeps us mentally healthy and builds family connections.

Know your family history. It keeps us close and connected.

Set limits on technology. Children do not know right from wrong in the technology world.

Children need time to play and create.

We all are equals, let us share and appreciate that thought.

I was born in Miner's Hospital in Frostburg, Maryland on January 29, 1957 to Faye and Maxine Kiddy. I have one sister, Catherine Anna (Kiddy) Miller who resides in Myrtle Beach, SC. I grew up in the small town of Lonaconing, Maryland. Lonaconing is a town in Allegany County, Maryland located along the Georges Creek Valley. Our area was called "crick" or creek because of the Georges Creek Valley. You were referred to in our tri-state area as from up the "crick" or up the creek. Sometimes the nicknames went as far as crick rats or crickers.

Lonaconing was a small mining town of about 1200 people. The people of Lonaconing were hard working people who took pride in their town and homes. This town was said to be named after Chief Lonacona, an Indian Chief who lived in this valley. This was a great town to grow up in with friendly people and a lot of surrounding open land to explore as a youngster.

Lonaconing was established by the Scotts, Germans, Irish and Italians. It was also the hometown of Lefty Grove. Robert "Lefty." Grove was a great left-handed pitcher who won 300 games from 1925-1941 in Major League baseball. He played professionally for the Baltimore Orioles and the Philadelphia Athletics and entered the Baseball Hall of Fame after pitching a lifetime career win percentage of .682. He also set an American League record of 16 consecutive victories. Lefty later returned to Lonaconing purchasing a bowling alley/pool hall called "Lefty's." There is a Lefty Grove Park in Lonaconing with much of the history of the professional baseball player. There is also a statue honoring his accomplishments.

I loved to play sports in my backyard on Douglas Avenue where I lived. The First Presbyterian Church of Lonaconing was a stone's throw away for me to worship and my elementary school of Central was an enriching place for me to learn in my formative years. Central was once a high school where my parents attended. Later a high school was built in Detmold, Maryland just about a mile and half from my home. Valley was for grades 7-12.

Rise Up

While attending school at Valley High, we did not have organized middle school teams. We had to organize our own play, something that is unheard of today in most areas. Each of the areas around town through the kids only, organized teams to play American football. You had to have a field to play home games and were allowed only six players on your team. The teams were Douglas Avenue, Rockville, Church Hill, Detmold and Charlestown. Our home field was my backyard at 26 Douglas Avenue and since it was my backyard, I was the coach and owner of the team.

I wanted to organize back in those early years. I can remember marking the field off with cones, washing the bases after we played wiffle ball, and even putting grass seed on warn areas. I was facility manager, ground crew and participant. I wanted life to be just right. I organized everything that was in site.

I wanted the Avenue team to have jerseys that looked great. I organized a carnival in my back yard with some of the players. We had ring toss, bottle knock down, and other quarter games. We also borrowed the neighbor's shed to create a haunted shed. You were blindfolded and we put your hand in ketchup to replicate blood and a bowl of pealed grapes for eyeballs. Our parents came and played games with the neighborhood kids. Our parents paid more than a quarter fee. We raised enough money to buy six jerseys for the team. The next day we marched off with the money to Ternent's Hardware store in Lonaconing to buy the jerseys. We did not care what color and found some cool looking white three- quarter sleeve jerseys with green stripes and numbers that looked like the New York Jets. Perfect! Only one problem, all the shirts had the same number "77" on them. Oh, what the heck, we looked good!

Each coach had to find his six players from his immediate neighborhood. I wanted all of our players to live on Douglas Avenue. A problem arose as we already had five players and then found two Lewis brothers from the top of our street. Well, you guessed it! I had to cut one of the brothers because all of the positions were filled by my immediate neighbors, except I needed one lineman. The one Lewis brother fit the mold of a lineman and the other was so-so. I kept the lineman and cut the so-so athlete. We were not a very good football team but we tried our best. No team had nicknames but somehow our performance led to other teams calling us the Avenue Pissants.

Needless to say, my first coaching gig at age 10 did not go so well. To add insult to injury, that so-so player in high school went on to lead Valley High School to a Maryland State Class "C" Championship in football, and was also the area leading rusher. He also went on to play football and graduate from a college you may have heard of in Princeton, New Jersey called Princeton University. I always wondered if my rejection of him as a football player gave him the drive to be a successful football player. He also became a successful administrator in schools in Maryland and West Virginia. Oh well, the other players became pretty successful people in life, but not in football. The Pissants folded after one season of sandlot football.

The free spirit of youth organizing a game of pickup or, as in this case, organizing a game, league, and entire season was heart-warming to me now as I look back as an adult. We had organizational skills as youth when we had not heard of an athletic director, equipment manager or even that most needed sports psychologist. Just get a ball, lay out some boundaries and have fun. Today we have games that park our youth on the couch in front of a computerized game of sort. **Set limits on technology. Children do not know right from wrong in the tech world.**

Graham Ramsey, former Director of Soccer Development for the Maryland State Soccer Association recently wrote an article, "A Time to Change," for Soccer Journal. Graham Ramsey talked about crossroads in soccer today. We are spoiled in the United States. On other continents, youth often have very little money and play with rotten old balls on parking lots to dirt fields, but have one common thread "Love of the Game." "What brilliance is created by play and it cost next to nothing," says Graham Ramsey. We see this in the U.S. on basketball courts played in urban low income/project areas of our cities. This is the reason the U.S. is King of the Courts in the basketball world. The Douglas Avenue Pissants had fun and I remember that fall season vividly.

Then We Ain't Winning

My dad Raymond Faye Kiddy was a Luke Pulp and Papermill employee for over 42 years. My dad told me later in life that he knew I was going to be a coach. I was eleven years old in 1968 and he took me to Piedmont, WV to see a cousin play basketball for Valley High School against Piedmont High School. Piedmont HS was an African American dominated team that won several small class West Virginia State Championships. Needless to say, they thumped Valley. On the way home I asked my dad if we would have some of those fellows on my team at Valley when I get to high school. My dad asked, "What fellows?" I said, "Those brown skin players." He said without hesitation "No." I responded by saying, "Then we ain't winning."

I played freshmen football at Valley High School. I loved the game. We were the Valley Black Knights. Our school did not have colors. We were the shades of white and black. The art world says black and white are shades of color. Whatever! I loved the game of football but after my freshman season I was standing 5'4 and weighed 90 pounds. I made my first successful coaching decision. I did not have the frame to continue with the sport of football.

The following fall I went out for the varsity soccer team as a sophomore. The soccer team was made up of nerds and football throwaways. Our coach Wayne Foote was also the high school art teacher. Wayne did not know soccer techniques, skill development, or strategy, but he was a damn good motivator. He worked hard at soccer and would even decorate our lockers with great art work and quotes to motivate us the day before a game. A ribbon in my locker said we are going to whoop up on the Indians tomorrow-what did you expect from an all-white town.

Wayne Foote completed a successful art teaching career only to return as an elected Allegany County Board of Education School Board Member. As a board member Wayne struggled with politics and also with the overall framework of being a retired teacher. He resigned from the school board after an ugly battle that went all the way to the state level. Teachers should never follow up a successful teaching career with politics. It gets really messy!

When I started playing soccer my education into hazing and bullying began. My football friends held me down and gave me 50 pink belly hits to my abdomen area until my belly was beat red for changing over to soccer. The inside didn't feel great either. This occurred because my so-called football friends were taught by their coaches to hate soccer players and the sport. The football coaches and players would call soccer players pussies and other foolish names to let us know that we were not equals and they were the dominant sport. This was a hard but good lesson for me to learn as a future coach. You should not be intimated by those associated with football and be aware of hazing in the locker room as a coach. The football vs soccer controversy did arise and reoccurred throughout my 42 years of coaching soccer. I have always learned to appreciate all sports and athletes in a sport. It also taught me to accept and appreciate all! Someday, America will accept and appreciate all women and men as equals.

I also competed in Little League baseball, Gold-Medal Basketball Tournament, and found another sport I liked in track and field. In high school, I ran the two mile and had some success until they folded the program my junior year. My sophomore year I qualified for the Maryland State Track Meet in the two- mile run. I finished 6th in the state out of fifteen runners. I was excited about my future in track but it was cut short because the school board could not find a coach. Our track coach decided he needed to stay home more often for obvious reason. This was a family crisis that did not just impact that family but also 33 track and field participants. To dissolve our track team crushed me and my spirits in my junior year of high school.

During my senior year of high school, I had become a pretty good soccer center forward. Scoring was becoming frequent and I also scored the only two penalty kicks I had ever taken in my life as of 1974. They were actually the only two penalty kicks I would ever take. At Valley High School I was named the Scotty Orr Memorial Award winner. The Scotty Orr Memorial Award went to the school's top senior soccer player. I was honored and it brought back memories because when Scotty Orr was alive, he lived across the street from me. He would tell me some of his soccer feats playing in Scotland when he was a boy. I also was named all Western Maryland Interscholastic Second Team All-Star Team that year.

Chapter 2: College Days

"Find out what you love and poor your whole heart into it."

-Ray Kiddy

If you are not happy, keep searching. Prioritize spiritual beliefs, relationships, work, hobbies and what makes you happy. Happiness is probably right in front of you.

When you are contributing to something larger than oneself, make that something better.

A small adjustment to your daily schedule will get you organized.

When you find out what you love, poor your whole heart into it.

When one door closes, pry another door open.

In high school I was an average student. I loved the social aspect of grades 9-12. I was in the top section of my class, but did not appreciate the challenges it gave me. My priorities were athletics, fun, and hanging with my friends after school. I needed a change.

After high school I attended Allegany Community College (ACC). I played two years of JUCO (Junior College) soccer and loved every minute of it. We were competitive those two years but had an even better season my sophomore year of college. The Maryland Junior College League of 26 counties and Baltimore City had divided the schools into two divisions (small/large). We played for the small school championship that year against Tacoma Park! It was a competitive game but we lost in the championship 1-3. This was the first I was involved in a championship game and it felt really good.

JUCO conferences should always be divided into divisions based on scholarships or size. Still to this day, the NJCAA (National Junior College Athletic Association) does not divide classification based on size of school but on scholarship vs non-scholarship. My best example is Montgomery College which has 20,000 students and Allegany College of Maryland has 1,800. These two schools were in the same classification. Would someone hit the NJCAA over the head with a hammer and wake them up?

My coach at Allegany Community College was Darrell Blank. He was a good soccer coach, excellent teacher, and an even better human being. Darrell got the most out of his teams and made us competitive. Darrell's downfall was that he never put time into recruiting soccer players but was happy with whomever came out to play. Later I will tell you about Darrell becoming my assistant coach at Allegany College of Maryland and why I should have fired him. "Shit happens and will," according to Forest Gump.

My athletic director at Allegany Community College was legendary basketball Coach Bob Kirk. Bob had won a state championship at Mount Savage High School coaching the boys' team in 1968. He continued at Allegany Community College by leading the basketball team to 2

National Championship appearances. Bob Kirk was enshrined in NJCAA Hall of Fame as a basketball coach and athletic director. He was a good leader of men and treated me like a son at ACC. He would see me after a game and ask me about the game and give me some advice as a student athlete. He once said I was the nicest person he ever met. Later you will learn how this all changed when he became my boss.

You Better Get It in Gear

When I entered college, I needed to become a better student if I was going to make it! I knew, through the organization of each day, I could do it. I scheduled all my classes in the morning hours, and studied in the library from twelve noon until soccer practice at three in the afternoon. After practice, I rushed home and studied until bedtime. Making a small adjustment to your daily schedule can go a long way in helping you stay organized. I think I was the most organized back in my college days.

My freshman year at ACC we had one of our best wins with a 3-2 upset victory over the Community College of Baltimore. Coach Blank said this was his biggest win in his two-year coaching career. "This is definitely the biggest win for me and maybe the biggest win ever out here," said Blank. "The entire team played well and just outhustled them all over the field." I had an assist in that game and we concluded the season with a 5-7 season. I had four goals and one assist during this 1976 season. We had nine players returning the following season and things were looking up for the ACC Trojans.

I worked hard during the off season in the weight room and tried playing soccer several days a week, indoor or outdoor. I went to Frostburg State College and played indoor with their four- year players so I could improve. Coach Blank upped our schedule to fourteen games and we were excited about the 1977 fall season. We closed out the season with five wins in the last six outings after a terrible start and finished with a 7-6-1 record and as stated earlier, played in the Small School JUCO Championship game.

That disastrous start was against Montgomery and Prince George's, two of the top teams in the nation. I scored five goals and two assists. Ed Carney, my teammate, finished with four goals and five assists to lead our team in points. Ed was named our Most Outstanding player that year. The award was well deserved. He was an all-round better player than me. I was awarded All Maryland JUCO Conference player first team and played in the All Region XX All Star Game on November 12, 1977. This was a great time for me playing soccer and I fell in love with the game of soccer and knew then I wanted to coach soccer as a profession.

I continued to play indoor soccer that spring at Frostburg State College. I was excited to attend FSC the following fall until I suffered a head injury in a car accident, May 1977. I was driving home that evening and another car swerved in my lane and hit my car. I was rushed to the hospital and received a plate in my head and 46 stitches. This concluded my college playing career. I continued to attend FSC as a student for the next two years. I missed playing soccer in college but it gave me the opportunity to focus on my grades. When one door closes another door opens.

Chapter 3: Bishop Walsh Opens the Door

"I am the least among you. Look upon me as your servant."

-Bishop James E. Walsh

Can we be as humble as Bishop James E. Walsh? Wouldn't it be nice if we could be like Walsh. Oh, to reach the point of mercy in everyday life as he did. A life well lived.

A life of mercy is characterized by compassion, forgiveness, and kindness towards others.

Coaching led me onto a path of love, passion, heart break, relationships, leadership and all the lessons I needed to learn about life.

Coaching is a very difficult profession.

An advertisement in the *Cumberland Times News* read that Bishop Walsh High School was looking for a varsity boys soccer coach. I was only twenty-one years old and starting my senior year of college. I only knew of Bishop Walsh High School (BW) from my high school playing days, as they did not have soccer when I played at Valley HS. Bishop Walsh was the only Catholic High School in Western Maryland, named in honor of Bishop James E. Walsh of Cumberland, a missionary priest imprisoned for 12 years by the Communist Chinese. What a great man! As I read the advertisement, I thought this could be a way to continue with the game I had learned to love.

Bishop Walsh High School was built in 1966 and opened the fall of 1966. The school opened with some 600 students and was run by the Christian Brothers, an order of Christian Brothers out of Pittsburgh, PA. The school was the consolidation of LaSalle Boys High School, St. Mary's High School, Ursuline Academy Girls High School, Catholic Girls Central, and Saint Peter's High School. When the school opened that fall, the cafeteria was not complete and the students had to eat lunch in the court yard on concrete blocks used as chairs. The story also was told that the school was cold due to an inadequate heating system and in the science labs they used Bunsen burners to keep warm. Despite these issues to open the school, overall BW was a beautiful three-story building on top of Hay Stack Mountain in Cumberland, Maryland.

I applied and received an interview with Principal Brother Mark Lowery, a Christian Brother in his late thirty's who appeared to have the private Catholic high school of 600 students headed in the right direction. They were adding soccer to the list of athletic sports and that spoke volumes to me. Brother Mark called me two days later and offered me the job for $325.00 for the fall season. Excited, I accepted the position. Remember, I am a college student in my senior year of college and the 9-12 students are only 3-7 years younger than me. In my eyes this could lead to something good or possibly great. Soccer led me onto a path of love, passion, heart break, relationships, leadership, and the lessons that were all I needed to know about life. I started working for BW on August 28, 1978.

When someone tells you they are a coach, you should bow down to them. I say coaching is the toughest job on earth when you look at the responsibilities. I know, I know, all jobs are tough. Try getting everyone rowing in the same direction as a teacher, coach or any kind of a leader is difficult. Just ask Charlie Brown!

Among the many and diverse duties of coaching are: providing instruction, and development for individual and team improvement; analyzing athletic performance; preparing student/athletes for competition; maintaining positive and professional relationships with students, athletes, and alumni; monitoring academic performance; coordinating all activities for home and away games, including team travel, meals, and lodging; scheduling practices and games; and participating in fundraising activities. Whoooo!

Ask any of my 1500 athletes coached over forty- two years and I know they will tell you Coach Kiddy hit on all of those coaching duties. I'm not blowing my own horn, just emphasizing the responsibilities of a coach. They all have to do it. Bow down!

Chapter 4: The Key to Success is Organization!

"A place for everything, everything in its place."

-Ben Franklin

Our work beginnings are fun to look back upon. It was interesting to think back at those years and remember how naive I was. I was going to change the world. Maybe I did change a little piece of the world.

There is no shame in being naïve.

The key to success is organization.

Keep your goals simple-1,2,3.

You can start something that is so good, it will never end.

Have fun at what you do! Laugh every day.

Monday was for organizing equipment, uniforms and a visit to Lion's Field in LaVale, Maryland. This would be our home field for practice and games during 1978 fall season. Lion's Field was a baseball/soccer field owned and operated by the LaVale Lions Club. My obligation to the Lions was to put up soccer nets and to line the field. This would become a ritual of nets and lines for most of my coaching career. Ask any head football coach if they ever lined a field at high school or college. The answer will be a resounding no!

Tuesday of the fourth week of August, I had my first practice as the head soccer coach of Bishop Walsh High School. Prior to this first varsity practice, Bishop Walsh had one junior varsity soccer season during the fall of 1977. That team was coached by Bernie Loar who later became Allegany County Commissioner.

So, I am now the head varsity soccer coach at Bishop Walsh High School. I was thrilled. My playing experiences were three years of high school at Valley and two years at Allegany Community College. I probably had as much soccer experience as anyone in Allegany County, Maryland. I had great training experience in coaching classes at ACC and FSC from 1975 to 1977, since I was now a senior at FSC. I was confident I could do the job. Why not? At age 21, I had a lot of successful playing experience.

I started preaching to the boys that the key to success was organization. We had to set goals for the soccer program, create routines at practice each and every day, and we had to be mentally flexible in the mind. Our number one goal was to represent Bishop Walsh soccer program in the best possible way. We needed to be both gentlemen, and athletes and respect all. We needed to show up on time for practice and get the most work we possibly could to improve within a two hour practice each day. Lastly, I reminded the lads that we were a new soccer program, and that we will have our ups and downs during the season.

High school soccer is an eighty-minute game and we must readily shift our approach! If we win, if we lose, if we tie, next game on! This is the point in time when Bishop Walsh started a boys' soccer program. What will we be remembered for when the program ends in time? Can we start something so good that it never ends?

We looked like a ragtag group with the players wearing whatever athletic-looking attire they could find in their wardrobe. Some players wore cleats and shin guards but most just had tennis shoes. In four days, we would open our first game against a soccer power house Mount Savage High School. We had two practices a day for those first three days. We just had a stretch and walk through on the fourth day. That afternoon we handed out uniforms and worked on getting everyone in cleats and shin guards. We were all excited for our first varsity soccer game in the history of the school.

I was nervous giving my first pre-game prayer. But once the ball was rolling, I felt the game of soccer fit me like ping pong fit Forest Gump. We lost the opening game 0-8 and obviously did not know what to expect. I didn't think we played badly but we were definitely overwhelmed by the Indians. They outshot us thirty-five to six. Next game on!

Mount Savage High School was coached by legendary coach George Bishields, who coached that same 1978 team to the Maryland Class 1A State Championship. I went to that state championship game against Middletown High School. I was proud they won for our area and then felt better about Bishop Walsh's first loss ever in school history. I replaced Coach Bishields at Mount Savage High School after his retirement and I remember the positive influence he had on my life. More about that later. Coach Bishields died in January 2024.

Is That the Pope in the Goal?

My first coaching season was fun and we did have several good student athletes. A total of twenty-eight players including Scott Wood who was a freshman. He played forward and had two older brothers who had played football at Bishop Walsh. Scott broke the football family mold and would become one of the all-time, leading scorers in Walsh school history. Craig George was the first goalkeeper I coached and he was a hardworking individual who had a short memory, possibly because he was shellshocked that first season.

We finished that first season 4-8 (1978) with a nice win over Bruce High School Westernport, Maryland. They were a member of the well-established Western Maryland Interscholastic League (WMIL). When I played high school ball for Valley HS, we were part of that league and Bruce HS was our archrival.

Bruce HS was coached by John Shaw who was also a well- known high school basketball coach in the area. We beat Bruce HS 4-3 in that last game of the season. They finished the game pounding our goal with shots in the last ten minutes. John Shaw said after the game: "You must have had the Pope in the goal." No, not the Pope, but a good agile athlete by the name of Craig George. I always appreciated George, John Duffus,

Marty Evans, Danny Gimler, Dave Kesler, Will Kirk, Bobby Miller, Doug Miller, KT Salem, Paul Schock, Scott Wood, and Craig Zimmerman. They led us in overall play that first season and babysat a rookie coach. Al Via was my assistant coach that first season and was a very positive support for the inexperienced Coach Kiddy.

After my first season as head soccer coach at Bishop Walsh HS, the Christian Brothers invited me to the annual faculty/staff Christmas party. The party was held at the Brother's house located behind the school. This was quite a set up with 9 recliners in front of the largest projection screen TV that I had ever seen. It also had a full kitchen and another large dining hall with a player piano. Rick Harris, our head basketball coach pretended to play the piano and we sang the night away into a drunken stupor. We were so caught up in the art of singing that no one looked out to see a foot of snow had fallen to make for a difficult ride home for everyone.

The coaches decided to delay the ride home and went over to the gymnasium and played the game of horse until 3am. What a fun, enlightened evening that ran into the early morning the next day! I fell in love with Bishop Walsh faculty, staff, students, athletes, and they welcomed me with open arms. Can a Presbyterian become a Catholic Christian Brother I wondered. Probably not, but as you will learn later, I become the Principal of Bishop Walsh. Wow!

Chapter 5: Anxiety Gains a Life of Its Own

"The mind is everything. What you think you become."

-Buddha

Sometimes our anxiety takes on a life of its own. We worry about everything. We even worry about worry. Love life and get over it.

It is OK to look for new challenges in your life.

Teaching in the same building with your athletes is a great advantage as a coach.

Find small gains in your life and build upon them.

Always focus on the task at hand.

My second season at Bishop Walsh HS (BW) found me landing a fulltime teaching position at the school. We had the chance to start practice on time that season, as did the public schools in Maryland. That date for fall sports was always August 15th! That was Wednesday and we had nineteen players come out for the team. I was excited and knew we could start to turn the corner in a winning way this season. We had a similar schedule but also added Saint Maria Goretti HS of Hagerstown, Maryland. I was always looking for a new soccer challenge throughout my coaching career, even in the early years.

On Labor Day, September 3, 1979, I came into my office after practice and was talking to Glenn Cross, our football coach, about his Saturday night win over Bishop Guilfoyle HS out of Altoona, Pennsylvania. Brother Mark came into our office and said our legendary boys' basketball coach Rick Harris had just taken a teaching/coaching job with crosstown rival Fort Hill High School. Brother Mark asked Glenn, with school starting tomorrow, what will we do with Rick's PE classes. Glenn, looked at me and said, "Ray, didn't you just graduate from Frostburg." I had just graduated in May 1979. I replied, "Yes" to which Brother Mark said, "If you want a job, you can start tomorrow." Yes, God works in mysterious ways!

Earlier that May, I had told Brother Mark that if I did not find a fulltime job this fall, I would be leaving the area. He appreciated me giving him a heads up and I think he knew we were building something special in boys soccer at the school. So, when he offered me the teaching position, I jumped at the opportunity, followed him to his office and signed a contract for $7,980.00 to teach for the 1979-80 school year. At age 22, I was on top of the world. Remember as a college student in 1979, one might make several hundred dollars in the summer working a part-time job. Now I was on my way with a fulltime teaching job and coaching the sport I loved.

Bishop Walsh HS was just one of the schools where I was able to teach and coach a team in the same building. In my career I coached a total of 13 different institutions/buildings. Having the soccer coach teaching in the same building with their students is not as prevalent as it

41

is in sport of football. Being in the same building with your athletes is a great advantage.

I hired two gentlemen I knew to officiate our BW soccer games. Actually, they were my friends. Steve Shockey would eventually be in my wedding, now that is a great call. Bacon Miller was the second friend who was my little league baseball coach once upon a time. Two great guys who were members of the Western Maryland Soccer Officials Association (WMSOA). We had these two guys for the next two years to give us great officiating, consistency and a little bit of a home field advantage. After two years the WMSOA made us go through them for assigning officials and it gave us a rotation of many officials. Steve and Bacon did a great job and gave me input at the start of our soccer program.

We struggled some in my second season at BW, but saw a lot of positive progress. However, the anxiety of decreasing numbers of players was on my mind! Can we build a soccer program here at BW? That first-year teaching, prepping for class and practice was a challenge. We finished the season 2-10 but lost six of the ten games each by 1 goal. Three of the other four losses were by three or more goals. We still had a lot of work to do!

Homer

The last game of the season was a loss to the St. Maria Goretti (SMG) squad 3-4 in an overtime thriller. SMG Athletic Director (AD) Cokie Robertson officiated the game to save some money in his budget. I agreed since we both grew up in Lonaconing, Marland. He was a famous local boys' basketball coach at SMG. His basketball teams competed well in the Baltimore Catholic League. Cokey called a penalty against us in the box to give SMG the victory in overtime (OT.) It was a bad call in my mind, but I did agree to let the SMG AD officiate the game. Nevertheless, I received a homer in more ways than one that day. The season finished very positive and we turned the corner in playing good quality soccer despite our win/loss record.

We were led by seven seniors with the likes of John Duffus, Danny Gimler, Pat Hymes (GK), Marty Mathews, Bobby Miller, Phil Policelli, and Craig Zimmerman. Scott Wood and Doug Miller scored six goals and two assists each and Miller was named All Area second team. God would show me in so many ways the benefit of hard work and good living for the next 40 years. An adventure was yet to come!

I also knew that Bishop Walsh HS was a good athletic school and a great academic school. I needed to pick up my game as a coach and academic instructor with a 6-18 coaching record and a real rookie in the classroom, I made some bold moves in both areas. In January, I enrolled in the Physical Education Master Degree program at Frostburg State College. The program would take me three years if I signed up for three credits each semester. Bishop Walsh would pay for 90% of the classes If I could earn a "B" or better. I could take one class during the fall, one in the spring and one in the summer. This would be challenging to take grad classes while teaching and coaching. I also would need a summer job since I was a ten-month employee.

In February, the girls' track and field head coach position opened. I applied and Brother Mark awarded me the job. This would boost my income by another $350 annually and pay for my college up front until my reimbursement kicked in. I started coaching track and field on March 15, 1980. Twenty-four girls came out for the team. I liked the challenge of coaching a second sport and another gender. To be honest I didn't need more prep and work! I now had a full teaching load, was coaching two sports, and taking graduate classes. Thank God I was young and had a lot of energy.

He's Not That Damn Good Looking

The track and field team was talented. We competed pretty well with the local competition. I was the only girls' track and field coach so I had to cover all events which is not an easy task. I had the captains stretch the team out and then I put up a list of all practice activities for each of the events that day. I rotated time trials each day and focused on that group for that particular day. The girls caught on and did an excellent job of encouraging their teammates when the coach was working with another group. Our strength was in our sprints and field events.

Since it was my first year, I heard a lot of the girls came out because the coach was good looking. One particular runner of whom I heard some forty-five years later said she thought the coach was good-looking and she would run track. "Then he made me run a mile the first practice, so I quit, because I thought, he was not that damn good looking." We were led by the likes of Christine Becker, Allyson Conley, Karen Delaney

Rebecca Jones, Jenna Perkins and Debbi Simpson. Our overall record for 1980 was 18-9. Not too shabby!

At the Athletic Awards night in May 1980, I had to speak about the teams I coached. I said that everyone wanted to know why I wanted to coach the girls team. Being young and naïve, I said in front of 250 parents that I use interval training at track practice. "I chase the girls for a while and then they chase me." Could you believe I said that? I ended up in Brother Marks office the next day for the inappropriate comment. He was pretty easy on me. Brother Mark was a leader of men and knew how to get the job done.

The summer of 1980, I started summer grad work. I needed 36 credits and the last six could be a thesis if I wanted to go that direction. The other option was to take an additional six credits. I thought if I could take six credits in the summer and six during the school year, I could possibly earn my Master Degree in three years. For some reason, I wanted to put this in the fast lane.

I also had taken on a summer job with the City of Frostburg, Parks and Recreation Department as a camp counselor. It was paying minimum wage at $3.00 an hour. My camp counselor job was fun and not at all like work. Each camp counselor was assigned to a playground that consisted of a field, basketball court, playground and a clubhouse that resembled a shed. I had to plan activities for the local children ages 7-15. On Fridays all the playgrounds would get together and go on a field trip to

Kennywood Amusement Park near Pittsburgh or go to see the Pittsburgh Pirates play baseball and other great trips.

The older kids were the most difficult to motivate and plan activities. The other counselors and I came up with a fun activity for the older kids. We would plan all week and on Thursdays one playground would go raid the other playground with water balloons. We rotated who would raid whom and the older campers loved planning the sneak attacks. It was a lot of fun for the counselors also. I finished the recreation job at the end of July. The City of Frostburg ended their recreation programs by August because all the youth and high school sports were gearing up. By that point in the summer, the city was probably out of money.

I picked up a soccer camp at Frostburg State College working for head soccer coach Ken Kutler and assistant coach Jay Hegeman. This camp was held during the first week of August. They held a Soccer Seminar Class entitled "Theory of Tactics and Strategy" earlier that spring. I attended the ten-week course and was very studious in the class. I think that caught their eye. I felt privileged they asked me to work their camp because they were top-notch college soccer coaches. Frostburg State played a tough schedule and competed with DI West Virginia University from year to year. This was a great soccer coaching experience for me and I worked their camp for the next three years.

I then only had one week to go before the start of my third soccer season at Bishop Walsh. I went camping with a couple of buddies at Savage River State Park in Garrett County, Maryland. This was a planned well-executed drunken wiffle ball tournament for three days with many hang overs and several leg and ankle injuries. When drunk and playing sport, the body reacts differently for some reason. The week of fun and games ended on Sunday. I was out of money and summer vacation.

I was scheduled to hold my first soccer practice Tuesday so I used Monday to recover from my week of fun and games. At 4:00 pm Monday, my phone rang. I navigated off of the couch to answer that old landline phone. It was Brother Mark, the principal. He said, "Ray, I thought you were coming back to teach this year." "Yes, Brother, I am." "Well Ray, we had our first faculty meeting today!" I had missed my first day of school for teachers in just my second year of teaching. I apologized and Brother Mark accepted my apology and I said, "See you tomorrow, Brother!" This is what happens when you are young and single. I just dodged a bullet and thankful I had an understanding principal. That could have ended a 42- year education and coaching career early.

Life constantly is changing. You have to adjust your organization plan to whatever life is throwing at you. Sometimes we are the cause of the changes in our life. A friend of mine said that everything that didn't go right in his life was usually due to self-inflicted wounds. Sometimes, it is just life making things interesting. Be positive and adjust your daily, monthly, yearly plan. Life, death, divorce, financial difficulties are all just a part of what we have sometimes thrown our way. Be readily flexible to endure strain. Bend, don't break!

Chapter 6: Keep Your Head Up

"Champions keep playing until they get it right."

-Billie Jean King

I always wondered if I was hitting the mark in my profession. When do you know you arrived professionally? Do I constantly demonstrate the qualities and skills to be a good coach?

Ten or more seniors will put you in the win column in the game of soccer.

You can learn from your colleagues-right or wrong.

As a professional, get to know your community.

Busy souls have no time to be busybodies.

I started my third year as coach with great anticipation. We had grown from nineteen players to 31! Brother Stephen F. Paul was our Athletic Director (AD). He was very supportive of all sports, but was really a great football fan. Brother Stephen asked me how the team was shaping up? I told him I thought our soccer program is progressing. He said I didn't know we had a soccer program. Not sure what that meant coming from my AD.

Brother Mark gave me the opportunity to hire a part-time assistant coach. I hired a gentleman by the name of Bill Garlitz from Lonaconing,

Maryland. Bill had been active in youth sports on the Crick while coaching his own sons who were good athletes. Bill would be my varsity assistant and also would coach the junior varsity squad. We had exactly eleven players on the J.V. team. We had no room for injury, but it was a building block for the varsity. I learned that 10 or more seniors put you in the money when it comes to breaking 500. Or almost 500!

I also beefed up the schedule and picked up Our lady of Good Counsel High School from Wheaton, Maryland in 1980. They were coached by Art Iwanicki. Art and I struck up a friendship that still continues to this day. We also picked up Damascus High School from Damascus, Maryland. We were on our way as a soccer program and people in the area were starting to take notice.

We also were the first team in 1980 to open our new stadium at Bishop Walsh High School. Our practice field became the outfield of the baseball field and we now had a new field. Both practice and game field were next to the school, so we no longer had to commute. Our students and parents worked hard on the soccer/football field thanks to great support from the BW Athletic Association.

I remember how in the spring of 1980, we had our physical education students take buckets across the field and pick up rocks and dump the rocks on the far side of the field. We did this in PE class for about two weeks straight. What a rock garden. One student said, "Let me get this right. We pay $1,000 a year to come to this school to pick rocks." I said,

"Yes, this is right." Tuition in 1980 was $1,000 for Catholic students and $1200 for all other students.

In 1980, we had twelve seniors on the varsity team. We finished that third season with a 7–8 record. This would be the last losing season for Bishop Walsh for the next forty years! The record did not represent our level of play once again, six of the loses were by 1 or 2 goals against some very tough opponents.

We were led that season by Mike Davis, Mike Lease (GK), Scott Duff, Jim Donnellan, Omar Fadl, Chris Fergus, Terry Lacy, Lenny Lapidario, Todd McKenzie, Doug Miller, Kyle Norris, Kevin Swanson, Troy Thomas and of course Scott Wood. Troy Thomas switched over from football to soccer and gave us great leadership and enthusiasm. Scott Wood scored fourteen goals and had six assists his junior year to finish third in area scoring.

Twelve seniors worked hard to keep us in games. We finished the season 7-8. I could see the trend that soccer was establishing at Bishop Walsh and we were well on our way because of the enthusiasm that that 1980 varsity team exemplified.

Close Quarters

Glenn Cross, Joe Carter, Bruce Widdows and I shared a small 12' x 12' office with four desks. It was tight, particularly with assistant coaches in there after practice. We had a great coaching staff in many sports thanks to great hires by Brother Mark, Brother Stephen and the head coaches. Many of our assistant coaches went on to be head coaches at BW and other local schools. Learning from coaches in other sports is a great experience. You can share a lot of information, drills, and philosophy simply by observing. Some of those great coaches were George Geatz, Gary Neus, John Alkire, Dr. Felipa, Bill Garlitz, Bob Harden, Bruce Widdows, and Rick Love. Sharing and bouncing ideas around with great coaches like George Geatz and Rick Love was a great learning experience.

Glenn Cross became our athletic director as Brother Stephen was aging and still teaching a full load. During the summer months Glenn Cross worked for a soda company in their warehouse and transfer building. Glenn worked loading trucks and whatever else they needed! Part of Glenn's summer money deal with the company was that Glenn could keep the money out of Bishop Walsh's soda machines. This consisted of four machines in the athletic area. Glenn and I became good drinking friends! As soon as our fall seasons were over Glenn would get the coins out of the machines and we would take the money to local Cumberland bars and drink the night away. This became a habit during the winter months.

We would park our cars near Glenn's house. He would yell to his wife that we were going to the local bar. She would yell back and give Glenn hell. He would yell back that he may not come home at all and off we went for a night of fun. Glenn and Kathy Cross remain my friends today! Glenn would later become an employee of mine. For me, this was a great time - an opportunity to get to know the community! As a coach, it is great to know your community, not that you have to drink with them.

Indoor Soccer? Bingo!

In December 1980, we started our own indoor soccer program. With more than thirty players, we divided into six teams of five players and one player coach. Dr. Felipa had goals made for us to fit the indoor game. We used a regulation size five ball since indoor was new to the United States and equipment for the indoor game was hard to find. If the fast-paced, soft-sided futsal was available back then it would have been perfect for our gymnasium.

Our gym time for indoor soccer was Sunday night from 6-10pm. Not exactly prime time, but it would give us a start of playing year-round. We kept stats for all teams and posted records and updates weekly on a gymnasium bulletin board. This was driving Glenn Cross the football coach crazy because he could see something stirring in Walsh soccer. This energized the lads and we ran the indoor season all winter until March 1!

Each Sunday, the community held a Bingo as a fundraiser for our school. Bingo would draw over 200 players who would sit at tables in the cafeteria and through-out the first floor of the academic corridor. When we arrived for indoor soccer, bingo was in progress with doors opening at 5:00pm. The entire school was filled with secondary smoke as cigarettes were approved, sold, and encouraged by BW. Without cigarettes, no bingo! When we entered the building, you could have cut the smoke cloud with a machete.

Ladies are City Champs

That spring, the girls' track team was very competitive. We needed to improve in the sprint area of the team and we did. We won most of our meets or finished in the top two or three teams. We won the City Championship Meet that consisted of Allegany, Bishop Walsh and Fort Hill. This ended Allegany High Schools eleven- year reign over the City of Cumberland.

Ten records were shattered in an evening that saw the Allegany High School take ten first places to six for the Lady Spartans. We made the most of second and third place to capture the three-team championship. Nancy Velandia led our victory march, winning the high hurdles and intermediate hurdles setting new records in both events. Record in the high hurdles was 17.7 seconds and 51.6 seconds in the intermediate hurdles. Other records set by the newly crowned champions were Kim Kirby in the long jump (16'6) and our 2-mile relay team 10.41.9 (Simpson, Himmler, Becker, Perkins). Jenna Perkins won the 400 for another highlight of the night. We finished the 1981 track and field season with a record of 25-3. Others who contributed that season were Liz Barillaro, Ellen Clark, Karen Delaney, Rebeca Jones, Jodi Norris, Kelly Rice, Donna Ross, and Carlie Stangle. Donna Martin was shining in the shot and discus. This was a big accomplishment for our team in only my second year with the girls. As the coach, I appreciated how focused the girls were while I was working with other athletes. Maybe they didn't need me?

The girls track and field was building in numbers and wins. Our biggest improvements were in distance, and middle distance. Jenna Perkins was winning the 400 and 800 meter race. Occasionally I would substitute Jenna out of the 400 and put her in the 200 meter run. If you ever ran middle distance, you know it can be a grueling race. They are in between a sprint and long-distance race. An all-out race!

Jenna was the daughter of Potomac State College head football coach who also owned a workout facility in Keyser, Wes Virginia called Perky's. Jenna worked out at her dad's gym and was a very strong athlete. Jenna Perkins is credited for turning around our track program. With Jenna, we switched from being a mediocre team to one that was top notch. She ran anchor on our undefeated two-mile relay team. As a junior, she broke the county record in the 800 with a time of 2 minutes 42.3 seconds. She also ran the 400 in 63 seconds flat. Busy souls have no time to be busybodies. She worked very hard at track and academics and went on to run track at West Virginia University. Today, she is a physician and leading a very successful life.

We had a lot of good athletes graduate in 1981. Interesting enough, some of the boys' soccer players wanted to be managers for the girls' track and field team. Why wouldn't they? The girls were beautiful and athletic. A high school coach needs student help as managers and statisticians.

Chapter 7: What is Up Around the Bend?

"Make your breaking point your turning point."

-Dennis Kimbro

Sometimes we are aware of our breaking point. We search for the light at the end of the tunnel. When we reach this point, find support, and be positive. Take a break from the negative.

When you are at the breaking point, take breaks from the negative.

The breaking point can be turned into your greatest victory.

Find a mentor to assist you along the way of life.

Always strive to better yourself in your profession.

The summer of 1981, our team physician was Leo Ley, MD. Leo actually had been a longtime physician for Bishop Walsh High School. Leo was not in good health. He was talking to me at BW the summer of 1981 and said there was one thing he wanted to do before he expired. He was quite a character and saying, "Expired," as he died. I laughed, and asked what he wanted to do before he met his Maker. Leo said he wanted to take a train trip around North America. I said that sounds exciting. He asked me if I wanted to go on this trip with him.

I told Leo I was broke. I was paying for graduate school up front and I had no extra money for a trip like this. Leo said if you take care of my luggage and play Yahtzee each night, I will pay for your trip. At first, I thought Leo was kidding. No, he was almost dead serious! I accepted and we traveled from Cumberland, Maryland, to DC., New York, Montreal, Vancouver, California, Texas, New Orleans, and back up the east coast and back to Cumberland, Maryland. The trip took eleven days and we were only off the train to sleep two nights. We stayed the night in a hotel in Vancouver, Canada and one night in the French Quarter in New Orleans. It was the trip of a lifetime and I enjoyed every minute on the train.

When I arrived home, Brother Mark called me! He said he needed someone to ride to Washington, DC to purchase a tobacco gun to water our beautiful new stadium field. He needed me to ride in a pickup truck with Popeye Hersberger for the purchase. I would do anything for BW and Brother Mark, so I agreed to ride along. Popeye was our groundskeeper at BW. He had thirteen children. When the dismissal bell rang in the fall and spring, Popeye's children would go get a lawnmower and cut grass until Popeye said it was quitting time. They were all good students and hard workers.

Popeye and I loaded in his truck to go to DC on a Saturday morning. Popeye drank whiskey all the way to Washington DC until we made the purchase of the tobacco gun for twelve hundred dollars. This gun would spray fifty yards at a time and be perfect to water our field. When we loaded the gun into the truck, Popeye informed me that he had too much to drink and he needed me to drive the trip back to Cumberland. I told Popeye the only problem was that I did not know how to drive a clutch. He said, "I will teach you." Popeye gave me a lesson in the parking lot before our departure and off we went. I ground that clutch for three hours. Popeye slept the entire way home and did not toss or turn while I was sweating bullets the entire trip home. I am glad I don't like whisky to this day!

We Can Create Something That Will Change Walsh Soccer Forever

In 1981, we knew this could be the season to turn boys' soccer around at BW. I had Bill Garlitz as my assistant/JV coach and a volunteer coach in Dr. Felipa. He was a great physician with an equally great passion for the game of soccer. His son, Raul Felipa, would soon be one of our great players. But my best addition to my main roster was that I started dating Lori Richmond. Lori and I grew up in the same hometown of Lonaconing, Maryland, but I was five years older than her. I started dating her the summer of 1981 and we became serious as the 1981 season progressed. Lori was a pre-pharmacy student at West Virginia University. She turned me down the first time I asked her out but she later came to her senses and said, "Yes" the next time I asked her. This was a break for me because she became the love of my life and still is today. We eventually married in 1985.

We went 12-4 on the season and Bill had a J.V. team that produced a winning season. That year the Lonaconing Hall of Fame recognized me for building a successful soccer program at Bishop Walsh. I was honored and still treasure that evening with my family joining me in that celebration.

I also created the Bi-State Soccer League consisting of the three Cumberland City Schools and four schools from Western Pennsylvania during the summer of 1980. This league was a very competitive league consisting of BW, Allegany, Fort Hill, and from Pennsylvania Altoona, Hyndman, Salisbury and Somerset. With the assistance of each soccer coach at their respective school we set out to help organize and provide a better and more productive soccer league for Western Maryland and Southwest, Pennsylvania. That first year, Allegany High School won the Bi-State League and Salisbury, the runner-up. But in 1981 we won our first Bi-State and City title by beating Allegany in our second game with the city foe 1-0. In one afternoon, we won the Bi-State and the City Championship. What a day for the Spartans, in only our fourth year of varsity soccer competition.

Our Lady of Good Counsel relationship was great from the start. We would house their players with our players in Cumberland and they would reciprocate the effort when we drove close to three hours to Wheaton, Maryland. Art and I would spring for the bill of the hotel room for coaches at the two locations. This would make for one crowded hotel room. When we went to Good Counsel, Bill Garlitz would take the coaches to the Starlight Bar. I would schedule Good Counsel as the finally of the season. This was a real treat for our coaches. Bill would get so drunk that he sat in a stupor at our table at Starlight with his eyes closed. He smoked Camel Cigarettes (non-filtered) in his stupor. We would move the ash tray at different places on the table with his cigarette, and Bill would still reach around the table and find the smoldering cigarette with his eyes closed and continue to smoke. Now that is the instinct of a nicotine addict. He was a real pro!

On our first trip we road on an old blue bus that was purchased by the school. We would be the maiden voyage for our old/new bus. This bus was ancient and the last row of seats was on a board across three supports. You guessed it, the bus broke down on Route 495 about 12 miles from Good Counsel High School on Georgia Avenue in Wheaton, Maryland. It was hot and we unloaded all the players on a grassy area off the side of the road. Very dangerous but we had no other option.

One of the boys was getting off the bus via the back door and said that another player on the bus was hurt. I ran and jumped into the back door of the bus, hitting my head and almost knocking myself unconscious. I was dizzy and had to sit down. The players concerned, came over to assist me in my dizzy state. When I felt better and asked about the hurt player, I found out it was a joke. I felt so woozy the rest of the night that I let it go and did not discipline the player who cried, "Wolf."

Good Counsel school sent us vans to get us to the game. Walsh sent a bus the next day to transport us back to Cumberland, Maryland. I don't remember ever seeing that blue bus again. A bad investment. Great plan but poor execution on the part of the athletic department.

Good Counsel beat us 3-1 and they had a goalkeeper who was being recruited by the University of Notre Dame. This was the level of play I was aspiring for at BW. Good Counsel was out of our league but I knew to be the best, we had to play the best. Good Counsel was a private Catholic school of one thousand boys back then and Art had fifty players in his program. The Good Counsel program was impressive and one I wanted to model BW soccer after.

We were co-champions of the Good Counsel Invitational Soccer Tournament that year. We beat Ryken 2-0 who later beat Pallotti 6-1 in the consolation game. We had a rain out in the Championship game against Good Counsel. Good Counsel beat us 3-1 at home that season so we, at BW, were closing the gap but the rain came and they named us GCIST Co-Champions. Scott Wood, Scott Douglas, Dave Dorsey and Neal Hovatter were named to the All-Tournament Team.

During the 12-4 championship season, we were led by Jim Alexander, Keith Crosser, Scott Douglas (goalkeeper), Dave Dorsey, Scott Gillum, Neal Hovatter, Chris Locascio, and Phill Thomas. Scott Wood was the rebel who switched to soccer. He was the big scorer who put BW soccer on the map in Western Maryland. Scott wood scored fifty- two goals in fifty- five games during his four-year high school career. He led all area scorers his senior year (21 goals) and had three hat tricks (three goals in a single game).

Our seniors were Matt Breza, Lenny Lapidario, Chris Collette, Jim Donnelllan, Chris Fergus, Pepe Medina, and Scott Wood. Dick King started that year as a freshman and was stellar on defense. The All- City team was represented by Scott Wood, Dick King, Lenny Lapidario, Scott Douglas, and Neal Hovatter. We had a successful season, yet, we were more like a good athletic team. I wanted us to be a true soccer/athletic team that played year-round. This was in my eyes, the only way to get to a Good Counsel level.

Philadelphia or Bust

In January 1982, I joined the National Soccer Coaches Association of America (NSCAA) - the largest soccer coaches' organization in the world. The NSCAA is now known as the United Soccer Coaches Organization today. This organization was founded in 1941 and headquartered in Kansas City, Missouri. United Soccer Coaches is the trusted and unifying voice, advocating and partnering with coaches at all levels of the game. They unite coaches of all levels around the love of the game and elevate the game through advocacy, education and service. This group evolved through the advocacy education service and growth at the grass level in the United States. They teach youth coaches who were dads that never played the game and wanted to learn. This was a great organization that I felt became too big for their britches thirty years later.

Bill Garlitz and I drove to the Philadelphia Convention Center for the NSCAA Convention. Bill at one time was a liquor salesman in the region of Maryland and Pennsylvania. He knew every bar and liquor store from Cumberland, MD to Philadelphia, PA. We left Lonaconing at

10:00am on Wednesday. We started hitting the bars for the five-hour drive shortly after our departure. We arrived at the Philadelphia Convention Center parking lot and decided to sleep in the car. We woke up at 3:00am. It was cold. I started the car and put the heat on. We woke up at 6:00am with the car still running. I don't know how we did not die from carbon monoxide poisoning.

We then checked into our hotel and had a great soccer learning experience for the next four days. The first evening, Bill found a bar called Kelly's and we drank there for fifty cents a draft beer. Bill brought a framed autographed photo of Lefty Grove, the great left-handed pitcher for the Philadelphia Athletics and gave it to Kelly's bar owner. We didn't pay for many beers over the next three nights. What a weekend! Wow!!!

I attended thirty-three conventions over the years. Sometimes, because I had very little money back then, I would write articles about NSCAA convention demonstrations. I would provide articles to Tim Schum, who was editor of the NSCAA bi-monthly magazine. Tim would send me $50.00 for my services. This was great help for a private school coach/teacher.

Charger Blue?

In March of 1982 our coaching staff was parading Scott Wood as a player who could play at a high level in college soccer. We sent out many information forms on Scott and his accomplishments. We had a call from the University of Alabama, Huntsville. Scott was interested in pursuing the field of engineering and UAH had a great program. Their soccer coach was interested in Scott and wanted him to come down for a visit.

Scott and I loaded up my Buick Skylark and hit the road to Huntsville, Alabama. It was only a seven- hundred mile drive. We drove all day and all night. We did some dozing in the car while the other person drove. When we arrived on campus we called the coach. He put us up in a dormitory on campus after he knocked on the door of two of his players and asked them to go stay the night somewhere else. Yes, the coach actually bummed a room from his own players. Is this really how you treat a soccer recruit?

The next day we had a tour of UAH and in the afternoon the coach asked Scott to lace up his shoes and scrimmage with the UAH team. They were the National Association of Intercollegiate Athletics (NAIA) defending national soccer champions that fall. It was eighty-five degrees that day in Alabama and we just left twenty-eight-degree snowy weather in Cumberland, Maryland. It was quite a workout for Scott. He did not feel he did well but I thought he held his own. Following the scrimmage the head coach offered Scott to attend UAH but warned him that he had a lot to learn and he may not see game playing time until his junior year of college.

Scott decided to attend Allegany Community College and play soccer there his sophomore year. He then attended West Virginia University and pursued an engineering degree. He became an engineer and had a very successful career in the state of Ohio. The Charger Blue mascot is a secret at the University of Alabama, Huntsville. No one knows what the Charger Blue represents. If you don't believe me look it up. Who wants to attend a school that doesn't have an identity with a mascot. Not me!

Track and Field Team Successful Again

That spring I was doing triple duty, graduate work, teaching, and coaching the girls' track and field team. The girls' track and field team was budding in numbers and wins. We were competitive in all track and field events for a change. We finished second in the City, County, and Area Meet. We just could not get over the hump to win big meets. A very respectable 22-3 season that was led by, Christine Becker, Karen Delaney, Mary Dougherty, Mary Ann Grooms, Kim Kirby, Karen Knippenburg, Donna Martin, Jodi Norris, Kelly Rice, Donna Ross, Laurie Simpson, Terri Simpson, and Karen Spiegelburg.

The summer of 1982 I enrolled in the All- American Soccer Coaches Camp held at Monmouth College in New Jersey. It was operated by the legendary Walt and Gene, Chyzowych brothers. The camp was organized as a youth camp and coaches' clinic. The coaches' clinic philosophy was that you have to be able to play the game and perform soccer ball activities in order to teach the game. During the day all of the coaches worked with Dan Chicarelli, a talented coach who put you through the paces. In the evening you were assigned a youth team from the camp and you would coach a team in practice, warm-ups and in the game. This was a great opportunity for coaches. A coach would observe you during the evening and give you great feedback. I loved it! After camp was over each evening you could go to a local bar(optional) with Walt Chyzowych, talk soccer and have a few pops.

Walt was a very successful soccer coach who later became the head men's soccer coach at Wake Forest University. Walt suffered a massive heart attack on September 2, 1984 and died on the tennis court at the young age of 57. Born in Ukraine, Walt played, at one time, for the Ukrainian National Soccer Team.

The summer of 1982, I decided to put my studies in high gear and attend the National Conference Seminar on Youth Sports sponsored by Towson State University. This could be used as an individual research and study in Health and Physical Education and count as an additional three credits toward my Masters. The course lasted four days at TSU. One of the clinicians was Dr. Vern Seefeldt of Michigan State University. Dr. Seefeldt was a leader in our country on youth sports. Dr. Cordts, my college advisor, spoke of Vern all the time in class. So, I was sold! It was a great four days of learning, focusing on youth motor development, education of parent, coaches and officials and psychological implication. I found myself discussing topics I loved with some of the leaders of sports. What an experience!!!

Coaching clinics, certificates and licenses are great and should be pursued by all soccer coaches at any level. American coaches need this benefit of coaching experiences since we started late to the game compared to our European counter parts.

Certificates, Licenses and Diplomas I earned over my career.

National Soccer Coaches Certificate in Association with Portland State University

PA West Soccer Association Coaching License "D"

NSCAA Goalkeeping Institute State License-Earned at Baltimore Convention

NSCAA National Diploma-Earned at Bloomsburg University

USC Youth Soccer Coaches Certificate-Earned at Philadelphia Convention

USC Goalkeeping Certification-Earned at Philadelphia Convention

Grow as a coach. Attend all the professional development and training you can.

Chapter 8: Promise

"I don't know where I am going from here, but I promise it won't be boring."

-David Bowie

As I stated early in the Introduction Chapter, I would become bored in a coaching position and moved on when we had success. The challenge left and so did I. I would not advise this for every coach, but I was never bored when I attacked the next challenge.

I loved my job when a team challenged my coaching skills.

Most of the time life is simple if we let it be.

Always be courageous as a family and never lose faith in God.

Hug your children today! Tomorrow may never come.

Walt Chyzowych and Dan Chicarelli invited me to bring my Bishop Walsh team to their indoor facility next spring in Philadelphia. I assured them I would. I am grateful for the invitation. The All American Soccer Coaches' Camp was a wonderful experience for me, one which wet my juices for the 1982 season.

The fall of 1982 showed promise with twelve seniors returning! Remember the ten senior or more rule? Still, we were a very immature group with no leaders. This was an average season with 10 wins and six losses. After winning our first City and Bi-State Championship in 1981, we finished second in both leagues in "82." The city of Cumberland was made up of only three city high schools-Allegany, Bishop Walsh and Fort Hill. Nevertheless, we still registered some good wins that season with wins over St. Maria Gorretti, Mercersburg, and Allegany. Good Counsel beat us 2-0 but again we were closing the gap.

One day while walking to practice I saw all the players in a circle and found two players duking it out over a girl. I was surprised that the two young men fighting had such a focus over anything including a girl. The entire team had little focus that season, but we were talented enough to pull off double digit wins.

Fortunately, we were led by some young players that would make for some great seasons to come. They were Jim Struntz, Raul Felipa, Mike Goodfellow, and Dave Dorsey. Scott Douglas did a nice job in the goal only allowing 7 goals in Bi-State play. Scott was 6'5"" and 190 pounds. He packed a punch! It was a winning record but I felt the 1982 season would have really put us in control of area soccer. After five years of coaching soccer at Bishop Walsh our overall record was 35-36! I really felt after this disappointing season that we were treading water and not moving forward.

Jim Alexander, Keith Crosser, Neal Hovatter and Eric Dorman made the All-City team. Neal Hovatter, Eric Dorman and Jim Alexander were named to the All Bi-State First Team. Dick King and Dave Dorsey were named to the second team. Dick King was a sophomore, but made First team his freshman year. This was a disappointment to me because I thought Dick did have another great season for us.

The 1982 season led to ups and downs but it did challenge me as a coach. I had to discipline my soccer team more than any other time in my young career. This can be frustrating, yet rewarding if you see the dividends of your work. I think we all learned many lessons that season and still pulled off a winning season despite set-backs.

The Pittsburgh Steelers hung a sign in their practice facility and locker room that just states, "The Standard is the Standard." This is a great quote to lead your team and to live your life. Most of the time life is just so simple if we let it be.

My studies in my graduate program were going well. I had already completed the professional education core course in Principles and Practices of Research, Developmental Theory and Experiential Growth and Curriculum Development. Nine credits down but still twenty-seven to go. I was glad to get the professional education core courses out of the way because now I could sink my teeth into the area of concentration in physical education and coaching.

Dr. Harold Cordts was my adviser and Chairman of Health and Physical Education at Frostburg State College during my graduate work. Dr. Cordts was a scholar, leader and a gentleman. I learned a lot from his teaching and guidance and I know that he was one of the reasons I fell in love with teaching and coaching. He put Frostburg State College on the map as one of the leading colleges in the country in physical education. I miss Dr. Cordts! He died too young due to complications associated with Alzheimer's.

Indoor soccer was going well during the winter of 1983. We were invited to the American Soccer Training Center in Bucks County, Pennsylvania. I kept my promise to Dan Chicarelli and Walt Chizowych to come to their indoor/outdoor facility with 18,000 square feet of field turf – the same size as the Spectrum in Philadelphia. Located in Warrington, Pennsylvania, the facility was owned by Chick Downham. I didn't know then that I would be coaching in that area for the Philadelphia Union Major League Soccer or MLS thirty-nine years later. Life is just one big circle.

We stayed overnight in Warrington, Pennsylvania and competed for a weekend. Team members were Jim Alexander, Dick King, Dave Dorsey, Raul Felipa, Mike Goodfellow, Neal Hovatter, Jim Struntz and Ryan Thomas. This indoor style of play was new to us, an official indoor area setting and we fell short in all of our games. Actually, some of the games were not even close. I thought we would have competed better. When it was over Dan Chicarelli said, "Sometimes these defeats are a great life lesson, but who wants to learn that much in one day?" Dan was right. It did teach us how far we still needed to go with our program.

We had a rough start that winter with our indoor soccer program. One of our junior players had two younger brothers that were very sick. One brother at age 14 had leukemia and the other brother had a brain tumor. The teammate and family knew that both boys' lives would be short lived. The boys said they were not afraid to die but they had a fear of loneliness. The brothers died a week apart. The parents believed the one son could have lived longer but died to be with his brother.

This family was so courageous during this time and never lost faith in God. This is when we doubt our Maker but my player and his family had a bond that was unbelievable. A friend of the family and funeral director, Bill Fredlock, said, "The family and community coming together has renewed my faith and my faith in others. The human kindness has just been overwhelming." The BW soccer team supported the family because we were all one now.

Hug your children today! Tomorrow may never come!

I happened to be close by in 2022 when the father of the two young boys also passed away. I attended the dad's funeral. It brought sad memories back as if the boys had died yesterday. But in 2022 this also brought back good memories of faith and trust!

Track Team is on Fire

Track season went well that spring of 1983. I felt confident as a teacher and becoming an established coach. The girls' track team had a season similar to the year before. We finished 22-5 and finished second place in the City, County and Area. We did establish several records enroute to the 22-5 ledger that season. Lisa Burkey set a school record of 12.5 in the 100 meters as a freshman. Donna Ross, Terri Simpson, Jennifer Lucas, and Christine Becker set a county two- mile relay record of 10:38 and area record of 10:41 that year. Jennifer Lucas posted a school record 12:41 in the two-mile run and scored 66 points which was the most ever recorded by a freshman at Bishop Walsh. Christine Becker was our team's Most Valuable Runner. She set a school record of 49.8 in the 300-meter hurdles. Tina Spano was also a member of the winning two mile relay team.

The student/athletes at Bishop Walsh High School were eager to learn and perform. I will always remember Bishop Walsh as a great time in my educational career. Brother Mark and Brother James were outstanding leaders at BW and I loved working for them. I also knew that I wasn't making a lot of money and I needed to complete my master degree and move on if I was ever to marry and start a family. Lori and I were starting to make plans for the future as she entered Pharmacy School at West Virginia University. Lori was very studious and lived in the library. This was great for me for when I would visit WVU, I could go to the library and study with Lori. We would study for five-hour shifts in the library on the weekends.

Chapter 9: Change

"If you don't use your power for positive change, you are indeed part of the problem."

-Coretta Scott King

I always embraced change. Change was like a fresh start to me. Never let change bring you down.

Embrace change.

A good leader should sit back and watch the dynamics during the first year of a new position.

Think outside of the box to get recognition for your program.

The 1983 school year started off with a new principal at Bishop Walsh School. His name was Brother Phillip Deporta. Brother Mark Lowery was moved to a leadership role in the Catholic Schools in Pittsburgh. Brother Mark had been principal at Bishop Walsh High School for nine great years. I knew I would miss Brother Mark but not until after Brother Phillip's first year had ended.

Brother Phillip did what any good leader would do and that is just sit back and watch the dynamics of the school during your first year and learn your personnel. So it was smooth sailing in 1983 for me and my soccer program. I also was named assistant athletic director that year to assist Sister Sharon Marie Slear. Sister Sharon was also our assistant principal and athletic director in charge of schedules, curriculum, instruction, and athletics. She had a full plate and needed help in athletics. I was happy to assist.

Bill Garlitz departed the program after two years at Bishop Walsh. He had done a nice job and had had winning seasons with the junior varsity team in those two years. Bill was always thinking outside of the box to get recognition for our soccer program. I hired Tim Rowan as the junior varsity coach. Tim was a soccer official in our area and had a stellar basketball and soccer career at Allegany College of Maryland. Tim also played college basketball at Western Maryland College. Tim hired his brother Joe as a volunteer coach. Tim admitted to me he did not know many soccer drills but boy was he a quick learner. The junior varsity team finished 13-1 in his first season. Not too shabby.

The Challenge was Great

The 1983 soccer schedule at Bishop Walsh had the most challenging season thus far with the addition of Mercersburg Academy, DeMatha and Rockwood. Our total soccer roster had grown to 38 players. We lost the last game of the season to Good Counsel 3-2. Our closest game in five years with G.C. How we ever met the challenge that season and finished 12-4-1 was beyond my wildest dreams. We finished 11-0 in the Bi-State and 4-0 in the City. We also finished 2nd in the St. John's Christian Brother's Soccer Tournament in Washington, D.C. Dick King was named the tournament MVP and MVP of area soccer in Western Maryland! Dick was awesome!

Raul Felipa tied the Bi-State scoring record with twenty-three goals. This tied former BW player Scott Wood. We also were led that season by Mike Goodfellow, Jim Struntz, Mark Amoruso, Craig Gillum, Ted Higson, Matt Pesta (GK), Keith Silva, Ryan Thomas, and Art Zais. Our indoor season was producing benefits and our reputation as a good soccer program was paying off and attracting some great soccer talent.

In the spring of 1984, our girls track team had slipped off a bit because of graduation of great athletes. We finished the season 8-11. We were third in the County and fifth in the area. A highlight was winning a triangular meet with Clear Spring and Hancock. We were led by Lisa Burkey, Maria Felipa, Mary Theresa Lippold, Donna Ross, Mary Shaffer. and Tina Spano. I resigned at the end of the 1984 girls' track and field season. I was close to finishing my Master Degree and Lori and I were planning on getting married following her graduation in 1985. By next spring I hoped to be planning my wedding and departing BW. I enjoyed coaching the girls over five years and have wonderful memories.

Chapter 10: Finale One

"God is still writing your story, quit trying to steal the pen!"

-Nate Paxton

We have all heard the term best-laid plans. The phrase is from a "Robert Burns" poem "To A Mouse." The plans we make are part of our organizational tool box. We must remember that most of the time we are not in charge of the plans.

A lot to learn but who wants to learn that much in one day.

Never underestimate your opponent.

Support each other in a positive way.

You make mistakes. Try not to repeat the mistake.

I like to think that God and Jesus have the greatest sense of humor.

The 1984 soccer season looked to be promising. I was contacted by a touring team, Tamedale, from England. They wanted to scrimmage us only four days after we had started the August practices. Since I never turned down a challenge, having played LaSalle and West Catholic of Philadelphia, Saint John's of D.C. and Good Counsel of Wheaton, Maryland, why not take on a team from England? It is just a scrimmage. It was great experience and the comradery was great. We lost 0-8! Again, "A lot to learn, but who wants to learn that much in one day?"

The fall season started with some terrible rains in our area. The rain was so bad that the area of Hyndman, Pennsylvania flooded. Hyndman is in a flood zone anyway and did get hit hard by the rain. Hyndman was to be our first game of the season. I called their head soccer coach Nelson Weaver to see if he wanted to postpone the game. Nelson was a great person who also coached wrestling at Hyndman. He was known to wrestle soccer players prior to the game in a playful manner. Not recommended for a pre-game warmup!

I asked Nelson if he wanted to reschedule the first game for both teams since his field was underwater for over a week. He said they only had had three practices before our game tomorrow but thought we could play since they had been working hard to prepare the field. He thought his players would be disappointed if he moved the game. Nelson said "Come on over and let's play" as if he would like to wrestle me. I prepared our team in pre-game practice that evening and said they only had had three days of practice and we were going on two weeks. We needed to play someone and this was an opportunity to get our first game under our belt. Our boys took the game lightly the next day as they should. As a coach, never mention the opponent's woes or that you feel badly for them.

Yes, you guessed it! They beat us 4-1 with their standout player Rodney Lehman scoring 2 goals on a soggy field. I was disgusted with our team performance but the blame really fell on me and my pregame talk about poor Hyndman High School! Rodney went on to be the all-time leading scorer at Hagerstown Junior College in Maryland. Later he would play for Jay Hegeman at Frostburg State University when I was an assistant for Jay in 1990 and 1991. Rodney was good that day and I think Nelson set me up, seeing that I was a very young coach. *Never underestimate your opponent. No matter how much it has rained on their parade.* Hyndman finished the season with eleven wins in 1984. Bishop Walsh 0-1 start.

Raul Felipa led us to a 12-3-1 record in 1984 while scoring 21 goals and 6 assists. We had seventeen seniors and six juniors. This was our first season at Bishop Walsh with no sophomores or freshmen on the varsity. Despite the slow start at Hyndman we won the City (4-0) and Bi-State Leagues (10-1-1.) Hyndman finished 9-2 in the Bi-State for a respected second place. We were led by Raul Felipa, Dick King, Rick Luzier, Matt Pesta(GK), and Ryan Thomas (10 assists). The entire team was outstanding and made me very proud of our overall soccer program that was now in its seventh year and my final season at Bishop Walsh.

In 1984 I also taught the players to support each other in a positive manner. If you make a mistake on the field, do not apologize for your mistake. Play free and be aggressive. Don't apologize for mistakes. You will make mistakes. Just do not make the same mistake twice in a row.

Penalty Kick Should Only Be Worth Half a Point!

During my first seven years of coaching soccer, the Federation of Soccer experimented with changing overtime rules for a tied game. One year they had all eleven players on both teams take a penalty kick. Another year they removed the goalkeeper from the goal and had you play overtime with ten field players. Are you kidding me? The team who won the coin toss had one hell of an advantage to take the ball first. The last change during that first seven years was to play ten minute overtime periods. Both teams would remove a player from the field each period until there was a one goal difference. This could go on until it was seven vs seven. Not a good solution for the health and safety of players.

This experimentation with overtime continues today. A simple solution to overtime is to avoid overtime. Play a regulation time and only give a half point for a penalty kick. A penalty kick should not be awarded a full point. This is simple, simple, simple-forty-two years of experience talking. Would there be holes in this change? Yes! There are holes in all change.

That spring, I was finishing my Masters degree at Frostburg State University and working on my thesis, a historical research paper of 30 years of Valley High School. This paper was on high school soccer at Valley from years 1953-1982. I recorded every shot, goal, assist, and save from every individual player at Valley during that time period. I used articles using microfiche in the county library, yearbooks and interviews with former Valley players. Remember, this was before the Internet and Google. The thesis included Valley's 52 game win streak from 1953-1959 that was recorded by Mikey Cochrane of Bowling Green State University. The fifty-two game win streak was listed as fourth in the country in 1980. It also included coaching records, scoring records, All-Star teams, and team records. This included the years I played at Valley so my thesis became a labor of love.

Suicide

The spring of 1985 I was walking through the main office at B.W. and saw one of my seniors sitting in the hot seat to visit the Principal Brother Phillip. I said, "What is going on, can I help you in anyway?" He said, "No Coach, this is something I can handle." I always loved my seniors' honesty from that "84" team and the way they handled their responsibilities.

My player had been caught throwing food in the cafeteria. He went to meet Brother Philip who had had his fill with this player and kicked him out of school permanently. My senior had already been accepted to a good college and was finished with high school, ready to move on. So I thought!

The player's mother picked him up and took him home. When they arrived home, she said, "I am going to the market, is there anything I can get you?" My player said, "Yes, please bring me a bag of barbeque chips." She left for the market. When she arrived home with groceries, she found her son had committed suicide.

They say a person commits suicide because of many reasons. I have searched and searched and still did not see any suicidal reasons or messages. I miss him. It was quite a blow to our school and to the soccer team. We tried to do anything we could for the family. We all attended the funeral together. This player was on my team for four years and I loved coaching him.

Players Will Make Mistakes. Guide And Love Your Players.

Lori and I were planning on getting married that summer following Lori's graduation from pharmacy school at West Virginia University. After my players death, I decided it was time for me to leave Bishop Walsh High School and to move onto another journey. Bishop Walsh gave me the cafeteria and court yard area for our wedding reception and Lori and I were married in the First Presbyterian Church of Lonaconing on June 1, 1985.

I left Bishop Walsh after coaching and teaching for seven years. My overall soccer record was 59-43-2. Not too bad after a 13-26 start. We had won 3 City titles and 3 Bi-State League titles. My overall girls' track and field record was 92-31. We won many meets. We won 1 City Championship.. We had finished runner-up twice in the County and Area meets.

That year, I moved on to Indiana University of Pennsylvania as assistant soccer coach and a candidate for a second masters in sports management.

As I walked out the doors of Bishop Walsh High school on June 1, 1985, I envisioned Jesus Christ laughing. God said to Jesus, "Don't laugh. I am bringing that cat back as principal of Bishop Walsh someday."

Chapter 11: Indiana University of Pennsylvania

"Welcome to the real world. It sucks. You're gonna love it."

-Monica from Friends

Much of coaching is in the prep work prior to the start of the competitive season. The team arrives the first day of the season for a workout. This may not be how I envisioned the squad. I look over the squad and think, is this all I have to work with. The mystery of coaching is exciting.

In the working world, you have to earn your space.

You should never put a lot of weight on an early loss or win.

Trust your players after you have prepared them for battle.

Suter Kegg, the sports editor for the Cumberland *Times Newspaper* wrote an article about me entitled "Kiddy Reaches Promised Land." The article was about my accomplishments in soccer at Bishop Walsh High School and how the hard work had paid off. I was moving on to coach in the college ranks. I began my coaching career as a single person. That status had changed for my collegiate debut.

In that article Suter wrote about a tribute by Ebbie Finzel, the onetime soccer All-American at Penn State, who coached teams to greatness at Beall High School. Said Finzel, "Ray Kiddy is a very fine young man. He not only loves soccer, he knows how to teach and to get the most out of his material. His teams are very well coached." I was humbled by Ebbie's remarks and thought I would always have to use those remarks as part of my mantra. Suter also said in that article that I was a good looking and hard working coach. I resembled half of those remarks. Hard-working yes!

I was just 28 years old. Lori and I were married and living in Indiana, Pennsylvania. Lori had taken a job as a pharmacist at a local chain and I was a graduate assistant working as an assistant soccer coach for Head Coach Vince Celtnieks. I also was working for the athletic department and doing research in the sports management program.

I started graduate work in the Sports Management program right after Lori and I came back from our Florida honeymoon, where we visited Disney World and Daytona Beach. We were married June 1, 1985 so after our honeymoon I thought that since Lori would be working all summer I might as well start working on my second master's degree. I took two classes that summer. One class was Aquatic Facilities Management, a Level III course, and the other was Physiological Basis of Sport. I earned an "A" and "B" respectfully. Not too bad since that first summer the honeymoon was not yet over.

The second week of August 1985 the student athletes moved onto campus and we began training. This was my first experience coaching at the college level and it was an eye opener for me. Our head soccer coach

83

at IUP was Vince Celtnieks. Vince was a hard-working professor/coach at IUP and I shared an office with him. It was actually Vince's office and he gave me a small desk in the corner. Ok, this was my space not yet earned, I get it. We began the first week of practice with a couple of 5K (3.1 miles) runs for the team. Vince participated and won all of those runs. Vince was 44 years old and beating all of the college age players. I was not too bad of a 5K runner. My best time was 17:42 5K back in the day, but Vince could out pace me any day.

Latvia

Vince Celtnieks was born in Latvia. Lativia is located in northeastern Europe on the east coast of the Baltic Sea. Latvia is the central country of the Baltic States (Estonia, Latvia, and Lithuania). In 1941, following the German invasion of the Soviet Union, the Germans occupied Lativia. The military occupation of Latvia by Nazi Germany was complete by 1941. Anyone not racially acceptable or who opposed the German occupation, as well as those who had cooperated with Soviet Union, was killed or sent to concentration camps in accordance with the Nazi Generalplan Ost (Nazi Master Plan). Vince was born in 1942 in Latvia. Vince's dad served in the German Army and could also speak Russian. This dual role kept his dad from being sent to a concentration camp. Before the Russians arrived, the family escaped toward Germany in Bremea.

When Vince was nine years old, his mother, dad, three sibling, and his mother's parents boarded a battleship to flee Latvia and head for the

United States of America. His parents had received a sponsor in America. Vince's dad was an architect and his mother was a certified teacher. When Vince entered middle school, his dad bought a house about a mile and half from American University in Washington, DC. His dad worked on large railroad and bridge projects in the U.S. His dad saved money from his construction business to purchase this house. Vince eventually attended American University (AU) and was an outstanding student athlete. He earned five letters in five different sports and is in the American University Athletic Hall of Fame for that achievement. The sports he lettered in at AU were soccer, cross country, wrestling, track and field and crew. What an accomplishment!

Before the 1985 IUP regular season started, Vince continued a tradition he had started at IUP. He loved to go to antique or garage sales. He would buy furniture and store it in his garage or basement on Oak Street. He then sold the remainder to students as they moved into the apartments or dorms. Vince provided a service and made some change from his venture. What an entrepreneur!

In 1985, Vince Celtnieks was in his seventeenth season at IUP and had compiled an impressive 131-73-15 record. In 1984 the Braves were 12-3-1 and ranked 13th in NCAA Division II. We opened with the Alumni game with eight former All-Americans, nine new players and ten returnees, including All-American Frank Paz of Philadelphia. Our varsity lineup featured Indians Andy Cole, Owen Dougherty, Jack Pacalo, Philadelphians Rich Betts and John Starkey, and international players Mark Van Den Boogaard of Holland and Ike Ezunagu of Nigeria.

Other returnees included Danny Gehers of Middleburg, Todd Hammond of Washington, David Hoover of Lafeyette Hill, Dave Markey of Wallingford, Tom Neslund of Chambersburg, Scott Russel of Pittsburgh, Todd Weaver of Bethlehem and Mark Yeadon of Bradford Woods. The alumni game was a nice warm-up of veterans and newcomers, as a tune-up for four Division I teams and three top 20 schools in Division II on our schedule.

American University-National Runner-Up

After a win against the IUP Alumni, we traveled to face American University in Washington, DC. We lost 1-9 and it brought us back to reality. **You should never put a lot of weight on an early loss or win.** This loss was against a Division I foe and former home of Vince Celtnieks. American University was led that day by Michael Brady's two first half goals.

We later learned in December of 1985 that American University would face off against UCLA in the NCAA I Championship game. The AU Eagles lost to the Bruins after four overtimes 0-1. The American University Eagles were led by the 1985 NCAA Men's Player of the Year winner Michael Brady that year. Brady won the Adi Dassler award from Adidas as the top player in Division I Men's soccer. American University retired Brady's No. 14 Jersey in 1986 and he was later inducted into AU's Athletic Hall of Fame alongside of Vince Celtnieks. Brady has served as the Head Women's soccer coach at Duke University and is now in his 14th season as the Assistant/Associate Head Men's Coach at Duke.

Vince was a tough instructor of physical education and fitness at IUP. He worked out constantly, jumping rope most days for an hour to classical music outside of our shared office, in the hallway. When he would give a written test to his class, he would hand out the test, place his stationary bike on his professor desk and peddle away looking over the students for cheaters while getting a great workout. Vince was great at killing two birds with one stone. If you witnessed this as his student, what would be your thoughts?

We started out the season Nationally Ranked in NCAA II. We worked hard. However, I think some of our players were working hard drinking alcohol as their college past time. We beat Robert Morris 5-1 putting us over .500 with a 3-2 record. This would be the last time during the '85 campaign we would be above an even mark. We played fourth-ranked NCAA II Gannon the next week and were pummeled. We never recovered after that game and finished the 1985 season with a 6-8-3 record. One or two games from a winning season can sometimes be so far away!

The highlights of the 1985 season included a win against Division I (DI) foe, West Virginia University, 2-1 and then a 1-1 tie with University of Pittsburgh. This was the first DI win and a tie in my first collegiate coaching inaugural season. We finished fourth in the West Penn Conference South Division. Several players received individual recognition. Frank Paz was named All Conference First Team, Todd Hammon Second Team, and Dave Marky was named Honorable Mention. We scored 25 goals and gave up 37 on the 6-8-3 campaign. I learned a lot about coaching older players and about patience with their other college commitments.

Halloween

In late October that season Vince heard the soccer team was having a Halloween party at the soccer house. Vince decided we should go so he dressed as a Voodoo with a mask and outfit. I took Lori with us. She was dressed as jailbird and I as a convict.

All three of us had masks so Vince instructed Lori and I not to talk as we entered the party. The beer was flowing with several kegs. At one keg, one of our freshmen was told by a veteran player to remove his hat because he looked like a pussy. I overheard the conversation. I followed the freshman player around at the party. When he would look at me, I would point to his hat in his hand and point to his head. As if to say, "Put the hat back on." The freshman player was tired of me and my mime shenanigans about the hat. He came over to me and said "Listen dickhead, I don't know who you are but knock it the fuck off." As his junior varsity soccer coach, I remained silent!

Vince walked around most the evening kicking people in the ass and then ignoring them. This explained that we did not have any fight left in us at the end of the '85' season. At the end of the evening, they had asked everyone to come into one room and they would choose the best costumes. Vince was selected in the top five to go up front and selected the winner. When they called your place out, you had to take off your mask. Vince whispered to me and Lori that when they called his place, we were to run out the back door and get in the car and ride away. Vince was selected the winner and we hit the road running so Vince never took off his mask. We never heard anything from the players or of them suspecting us attending their party. But the way I witnessed the team putting away the beer, it proved what I thought about our partying during the season. These were seasoned drinkers. Vince, Lori, and I were also seasoned drinkers so after the soccer party we then went to a cross country party to continue the night.

I only coached at IUP during the 1985-86 school year. I continued in the spring and took the team to several spring games. My first college coaching experience with Vince was wonderful. He was patient and gave me a lot of responsibility. Vince and his family, his wife Jen and his children Dionna, Bill, and Chris, have remained great friends of our family over the years. Vince and I have attended over twenty-plus National Soccer Coaches Conventions together. He is a great friend and mentor on whose advice I have always relied.

Trust your players after you have prepared them for battle.

Chapter 12: Two Years-Three College Teams

"Do your best. That is success."

-John Wooden

I was fortunate to be coaching when colleges were adding the sport of women's soccer.

The facilities were not in place, but college administrators could see the growth of women's sports.

A class act is a person displaying impressive and stylish excellence.

Women in sports have seen significant growth, yet continue to face challenges related to gender equity.

During the 1985 winter and 1986 spring season I was working as assistant soccer coach at IUP. Westminster College is located in New Wilmington, Pennsylvania. They advertised for a head soccer coach for the fall of 1986. Westminster College is a private, liberal arts college. It is affiliated with the Presbyterian Church. The student population was about 1300 students back then. I wanted to apply for the position because I knew Vince Celtniecks would be coaching for a long time at IUP.

Westminster was a NCAA Division II and Western Pennsylvania Athletic Conference (WPISC) District 18 athletic program. They had had a club soccer program for nine years and were ready to move on to the varsity level during the fall of 1986. The club team had recorded a 4-4 record against area junior varsity teams.

I discussed the position with Lori and Vince and they agreed I should go for it. I applied for the position and received a call for an interview by Joe Fusco who was Westminster College athletic director and head football coach. He had arranged for me to stay in a hotel the night before my interview near New Castle, Pennsylvania at a nice hotel that was across from an Amish Cheese Company building. I went to bed around 10:00 pm to get a good night's sleep before my interview the next day at 9:00 am . All night long I heard horse hoofs and wagon wheels coming out of the Amish Cheese Company. They were making deliveries. It must have been a thriving business, because they kept me awake all night. This was an interview night(mare) of hoofs.

I worked through the interviews with Dr. Fusco and some other committees he had set up. I drove home that day and just wanted to get back to Indiana to nap. I was too sleepy to know if I did a good job during the interviews or not. As it turned out, Dr. Joe Fusco called me the next week and offered me the position. I met with Joe the following week and I signed a contract with a modest salary to be the next Westminster College head soccer coach - my first head college coach position. I was excited. Westminster also offered me housing on campus where many of the instructors live.

Lori and I were excited about the upcoming move. Lori's aunt and uncle lived in Poland, Ohio just 20 miles northwest of Westminster. Lori went to work on finding a job and was successful finding a pharmacist position with a chain in Shenango Township. We both now had a new start in a new area with family ties. Life could not be better.

I started working on recruiting for Westminster College and continued finishing my responsibilities at IUP. I would travel from IUP to Westminster to practice my new team two days a week. Lori moved in with her aunt and uncle and began work in Shenango Township. We both were busy for the next six weeks along with packing for our move.

This Just Isn't Fair!

After my six weeks of practice at Westminster, students were ready to go home for the summer and I really needed to hit the recruiting trail hard. I went in to meet with Dr. Fusco about arranging transportation for recruiting travel. Dr. Fusco gave me some bad news. He informed me that the housing they had promised me was no longer available. It had been offered to a biology instructor they had hired at Westminster. That person received my housing because housing goes first to professors over coaches. I told Joe this was quite a blow and I would talk to him later after I discuss it with my wife.

Lori and I got a realtor and began looking for other housing. We both decided that we needed a plan B because housing around the area was more than we could afford and we were both tired of apartments. We decided to pull the plug on Westminster College and her job. I called

Dr. Fusco and resigned after just six weeks as a head college soccer coach following the weekend. Lori and I had to move quickly to come up with plan B.

Instead of focusing on packing and the move Lori and I began looking for other work. I flew to Jacksonville, Florida and interviewed for a Boys and Girls Club athletic director position. Boys and Girls Club of America flew me in for the interview. Following the interview, I rented a car and drove 249 miles to Cuthbert, Georgia to interview for a head women's soccer coaching position at Andrew College. Andrew College is a private liberal arts college associated with the United Methodist College.

Following the Andrew College interview I drove 161 miles to the Atlanta, Georgia airport. From there I caught the flight from Jacksonville, Florida to Pittsburgh, Pennsylvania, which had been provided by the Boys and Girls Club of America. Such is the life of an American Soccer Coach. I wonder if this is how Nick Saban did it when he got the Alabama job.

When I arrived home from the interview Lori had already landed a job at a chain drug store as a pharmacist in Churchville, Maryland. Lori is more marketable at this time and needed to drive/fly less for interviews. Lori set this up in the store, where she had been working in Indiana, Pennsylvania. Baltimore, Maryland area was clearly where I need to set my sites on a job. At least we were zeroing in on the southeast coast.

I landed a job as a recreation supervisor for the Maryland Department of Juvenile Services. I also found a part-time head women's college soccer coaching job at the Community College Baltimore Campus (CCBC). This was a NJCAA school in the Maryland JUCO Conference. Lori and I found a townhouse to rent in Owings Mills, Maryland and so we finished the packing and drove 220 miles to our new home. We moved June 19th, 1986, the day that the world had found out Len Bias had died of a cocaine overdose. This was two days after he was selected as a second overall pick of the Boston Celtics in the 1986 NBA draft. A tragic day for American college basketball fans. I remember it all too well.

Gary Keedy was the athletic director at Community College Baltimore Campus (CCBC). He was an outstanding athlete from Keyser, West Virginia. Keyser, WV is not far from my hometown of Lonaconing, Maryland. He offered me the job and I had very little time to recruit for the team. I jumped straight into the role of head college coach—my second time coaching at the college level, if you count the six chaotic weeks during a housing crisis at Westminster College in Pennsylvania. Not the typical head college coaching debut.

On the first day of practice at CCBC I had eleven players show up. Not one returning player from the year before but at least there was one goalkeeper. The only way to recruit at this point was to put up fliers around campus. I made up the fliers and took a three-mile jog around campus with my trusty stapler to every building and hallway bulletin board. Not one other girl contacted me! At least I did get a run in for the day, around campus.

Obviously, you are going to struggle as a team with just 11 players. The girls worked hard and gave their best. I had to tone-down our practice through out the season so we would not suffer any injuries. Normally as a soccer coach you would lighten the workload at practice during the second month of the season. At CCBC I had to lighten the workload up, during week two. We struggled through the season without a win (0-8). My first college coaching season did not produce one win nor one tie. The highlight of the season was during our last game against Nationally Ranked Anne Arundel Community College. They scored early on a corner kick but only beat us 1-0. AACC went to the Nationals that fall. I was proud of my girls. They worked hard and fought through several injuries during the fall. We never went down to ten players at the beginning or end of any game. A moral victory. This was the only no-win season I ever suffered during my 42 year coaching career. And boy did I suffer!

I Will Probably Get Fired!

Following the 1987 soccer season, Gary Keedy called me to asked me to come in for an evaluation. I thought I could get fired today. The only response I could give Mr. Keedy was that I had given it my best! Sometimes in coaching, through lack of chemistry or talent, it just does not work out. In this case it was lack of numbers! That is an answer the AD does not want to hear because you are the recruiter.

I walked into Gary Keedy's office and he stood up and shook my hand and asked me to sit down. Here it comes!! He went over all the positive coaching tributes he had observed during the past fall and said he thought I did a great job. I thought, "Here it comes." "I want you to come back if you would like and I am excited about next season after you have an entire school year to recruit players." I was a little light headed because I did not see this coming. "You want me to come back after going 0-8." "Yes, you gave your best." Hey, that was my line. He did follow up with, "If you have another 0-8 season you may want to find another profession." We both laughed. What a class act of an athletic director I had in Gary Keedy. I never returned to coach at CCBC but I will never forget the humility of that season and Mr. Keedy. Gary was inducted into the CCBC Hall of Fame on December 2, 2022. From that point on I always knew what a class act is after working for Gary Keedy!

During the winter of 1987, I attended the NSCAA Convention in Boston. The NSCAA Journal had a program at the Convention to earn money for coaches attending. You could attend a session, write a recapitulation of the session, submit to the Journal, and they would pay you fifty dollars. I wrote up several articles and made one hundred and fifty dollars. This was a way to offset the convention expenses and also gain some exposure with the NSCAA and my fellow coaches.

One article I provided was a session by Tom Fleck who presented a session adapted from material on "Heading the Soccer Ball" contained in the NSCAA Advanced National and National Level Diploma Course Syllabus. Tom Fleck was the head soccer coach at Lehigh University and later became General Manager of the Philadelphia Fury in the North American Soccer League. He also served on the Board of Directors of the United Soccer Coaches (formerly the NSCAA) and was president in 1984-85. He was a well-educated soccer coach and had a great sense of humor. I have loved all of Tom Flecks sessions I attended over the years.

The Gators

While attending the NSCAA Convention in Boston I saw an ad that the College of Notre Dame in Baltimore was looking for a head women's coach. I thought, "Why not apply and see if anyone one is out there looking for a college coach with an overall college coaching record of 0-8." Guess what, they were. Betsy Alden the Notre Dame athletic director called me to come in for an interview. The campus was small, attended only by women.

I interviewed for the job and Betsy Alden awarded me the position a week later. We were already behind in the recruiting season but I would do my best to put together a competitive squad. Betsy also made me aware that our practice field only had one soccer goal! What? We would play our home games at our neighbor's field, Loyola University. The College of Notre Dame and Loyola University had an agreement to share athletic facilities and the library.

Today the College of Notre Dame is called Notre Dame of Maryland University. It offers certificate undergraduate, and graduate programs for women and men. NDMU offers eight women's sports and five men's sports.

We started our training in August of 1986 on our lone soccer goal field. The team consisted of thirteen players and, once again, only one goalkeeper. I was wondering if I was ever going to have a full year to recruit at the college level. The ladies worked hard but it was hard to compete with so few players. They gave it their all and we finished 3-3-2, a satisfying season for never practicing on our home field and only having 13 players.

Betsy Alden was satisfied with the job I did! She offered me the head women's tennis coaching position. I played tennis recreationally but not at the high school or college level. We never had a tennis team at Valley High School. I told Betsy I would love it if I could hire a good assistant coach. She said we already have a Catholic nun at the College who wants to be the assistant. She said the nun is an excellent teacher at the College and plays a lot of tennis. I said, "Great-I will do it. " It turns out the nun was Sister Sharon Marie Slear. I had worked with Sister Sharon at Bishop Walsh. She eventually became the athletic director at BW and I was her Assistant Athletic Director in 1983 and 1984.

I loved working with Sister Sharon and we had a very competitive team. We had ten team members. The ladies competed well and we finished in third place in our conference, with several players named All Conference.

When Montrose School closed, my position as Recreation Supervisor ended. I began working as a personnel specialist for the State of Maryland. I was part of a study to evaluate state worker positions and assist in revamping the employee ladder in recreational, nursing and other leadership roles. I would ride the train from Owings Mills to downtown Baltimore each day. College of Notre Dame was looking to grow and was in the process of building a new Athletic/Physical Education building. Maybe this would be a good home for me!

Sister Sharon Marie Slear had an illustrious thirty- four year career at NDMU. She created many educational programs to meet the University's needs. Sister Sharon was a College of Notre Dame graduate receiving the Maryland Alumnae Award in 1965. She was also named one of Maryland's top 100 women in 1999, 2006 and again in 2009. This placed her in the Maryland's top 100 Women Circle of Excellence. We had a good working relationship and I was honored to be part of a women's tennis team.

Betsy Alden went on to be a great leader in U.S women's athletics. She was athletic director at the College of Notre Dame and also Webster University, San Francisco State University, and Ithaca College. She later became President of the National Association of Collegiate Women's Athletic Administrators.

I often think about these two remarkable women in leadership roles whom I had the privilege of working with during the 1987–88 school year at the College of Notre Dame. I know they shaped my coaching and leadership role later in my career. Respect of the female athlete was something I always appreciated during my forty-two year coaching career. I know that Betsy Alden and Sister Sharon Marie Slear helped shape my view of female athletes.

Chapter 13: Gun Shy

"Do something you're not ready to do. In the worst case, you'll learn your limitations."

-Marissa Mayer

If we lose, we will learn from our defeat. If we win, we will share our victory.

Any spouse always needs to be aware of the other half and how your work life affects the family.

Family monthly meetings help with the flow of life.

Savor the winning seasons, even though it is not why coaches are in the business.

After finishing the last two seasons as a College Head Coach with a record of 3-11-2, I was gun-shy and decided to take two years off as a soccer coach in the Baltimore area. I was working as a personnel employee for the State of Maryland and we were living in the Owings Mills/ Reisterstown area. Lori and I were expecting our first child in September of 1990.

In January of 1990 we looked to move closer to home for more family support as we started our own family. We were in need of both my parents and Lori's parents. Lori's parents, Bill and Judy Richmond, have been rockstars for our family. They have always been there for us and they have always treated me like one of their own.

Our thinking was we needed to be closer to home to have family support. I applied for a Parks and Recreation Director position for the City of Frostburg. I was offered the position and we headed home. Frostburg is about nine miles from our hometown, Lonaconing, Maryland. It is a city in Allegany County and the home of my alma mater, Frostburg State College (FSC).

Shortly after we moved to Frostburg and I was working for the City of Frostburg, Dr. Johnston (Jay) Hegeman, the Head Men's soccer coach at FSC, called me. Jay was an instructor at FSC and was a storied soccer player. Jay asked me to be a part-time assistant coach on his staff. I was excited for the offer because Jay and I were friends from working soccer camps at FSC in the past. We had also played in the adult soccer league in Allegany County over the years.

Lori and I discussed Jay's offer that evening. This was a big decision. Our first child was due in September 1990, mid-season of the FSC fall soccer season. After my last two experiences at the college level, it was obvious I was a better college assistant than head coach. Lori agreed this was a good opportunity for me and I accepted the assistant position at FSC.

Jay was an excellent coach. He was subtle and brief. His halftime talks were to the point of three things we needed to focus on. Then he had each of the assistants give their input. Jay always said I was loquacious. That is a person who talks a lot, often about stuff that only they think is interesting. That is me-if the fu shits wear it!

Carl Rees was the other assistant coach. Carl was a graduate assistant at Frostburg State College. He is originally from Bebington, England. Carl was a four- year starter at Hartwick College. He led Hartwick in scoring his senior year with 10 goals and four assists. He also received a spot on the Soccer America All-Freshman team in 1984.

We had a great 1990 season at FSC, going 14-5-1 and ECAC South Region Championship Runner-up. That Bobcat team won ten games in a row, at one point, before hitting a bad patch near the end of the season. We outscored our opponent 66-17.

Ross

Lori and I had out first child Ross Alan Kiddy on September 13, 1990 at 7:00pm. While we were so excited to be parents and to start our family, that fall soccer season took its toll on Lori with me working as Parks and Recreation Director and coaching at FSC. After finishing the regular season 13-4-1 we were awarded to play in the ECAC South Region Championship for NCAA Division III schools. Everyone was excited except Lori. I totally understood how hard this fall had been on Lori basically raising our first born for a month and half without me.

Any spouse and especially coaches always need to be aware of the other half and how your work life affects the family. You have to be organized together, when career moves impacts coaching or work. My oldest son Ross and his wife Erin, have a family meeting each month to go over their household organization and most important their family budget. What a great idea.

Our first game in the ECAC South Region Championship was at home against Gettysburg College whom we tied 2-2 during the regular season. We were lucky to tie that first game so I told Lori the season could very well end with the Gettysburg game. She was excited about an expected loss. I saw Lori pushing Ross in a stroller around Loop Road near our field. She was ten minutes late. We had already gone up 3-0 in the first ten minutes.

We did not have a visible score board so Lori did not know the score when she arrived. I walked over to the fence sheepishly to say hello to Lori and Ross. Lori asked the score and I told her we were up 3-0. She departed the game immediately. We went on to win 4-1 over Gettysburg. I went home after the game to find Ross asleep and Lori lying flat on the bed crying. She had suffered enough and I knew it. I consoled her and she asked, "What is next?" after she stopped crying. I told her Jay will call me later to tell me what would be our next game.

A Dog's Life

Ugh! Jay called me that night and said we are departing for Wilkes College in Wildes-Barre Pennsylvania in the morning to play in the ECAC South Region Championship game. Lori hung in there and gave me her blessings in the morning as we departed for the Championship Game. Lori did know this next game would close the 1990 fall season and was optimistic. She always hung in there with me through rain or shine. I love that woman.

We lost the next day in a hard-fought game against Wilkes College 0-2! That 1990 season was the spark I needed for my coaching career. I enjoyed bonding with the players, Jay and Carl. I did have a lot of fun with Carl at the expense of our head coach, Jay. Jay was a great coach and I learned a lot from him. Jay was tight with his budget money and Carl and I gave him the name Jay Hegestein. Jay always focused on the game. The next day, Carl and I snuck out for a beer and talked about how we'd do things if we were the head coach. And there was Jay's dog, UB, who did victory rolls after each win. You never saw a dog roll so much during our ten game win streak. That dog had to have fleas for months after that win streak.

Rahlo and Pete Titus were our goalkeepers during that 1990 season. Mark Urban had the most goals with 12, followed by Rocky Reed 11, and Derick Woodward with 10. The three scored half of our 66 goals.

Carl Rees went on to have an outstanding coaching career at Fairfield University. He is the all-time winningest coach in Fairfield athletics with 246 wins. Under his guidance, the Stags reached double figures in the win column 11 times during his career including 15 wins in 1998 15-4-1 and in 2006 15-6-1. I find it interesting that he tied our 15 wins at FSC in 1990, twice, while at Fairfield. Those type of seasons do not come along every fall. As a coach you have to savor the winning season, even though it is not why coaches are in the business.

As for Dr. Johnston (Jay) Hegeman, not enough can be said. Jay was an outstanding player and coach at FSU. His FSU career spanned four decades, starting as a player in the early 1970's and finishing as the program's head coach in 2001. Jay led the Bobcats to a 191-103-15 record in his 16 years at the helm. The Bobcats appeared in two NCAA, Nine Eastern College Athletic Conference (ECAC) and five Allegheny Mountain Collegiate Conference (AMCC) Tournaments

Jay led his teams to a combined six ECAC (3) and AMCC (3) Tournament titles and was named the AMCC Coach of the year, three times. Hegeman's teams won 10 or more games in nine of his 16 season while his 1991 and 1997 teams hold the school record with 17 wins in a season.

I will always consider Jay a friend, colleague and mentor. I am very fortunate he was part of my life.

Ray's Early Years in Elementary School

Ray competes for the two-mile county championship his sophomore year of high school

Ray's high school senior year

Valley High Award Winners

Here are the major sports award winners at Valley High School who received their trophies at the annual All-Sports Banquet recently at the Barton American Legion. In front row, from left, are Kevin Green, who was cited for his performance in wrestling; Denise Rinker, cheerleading; Sally Snyder, girls' basketball; and Ray Kiddy, soccer. In back row from left are "Lefty" Driesell, head basketball coach at the University of Maryland who was guest speaker; Kim Myers, football; Tom Wilt, baseball; Danny Duncan, football and basketball; and Dr. Leo Ley, the master of ceremonies for the evening.

Valley High School top athletic award winners in 1975

Allegany Community College 1976 Men's soccer team. Ray is number 25 standing next to Coach Blank in second row on the far left

Bishop Walsh High School court yard under construction in 1966. Kiddy served as teacher, coach, athletic director, had his wedding reception in the same court yard, and later became principal.

BISHOP WALSH SOCCER

1st Row   Left to Right
Todd McKenzie, Mark Warren, Marty Evans, Andy Hare, Matt Barazio, Lenny Lapodario, Doug Miller.
2nd Row
Chris Collett, Scott Jewel, Doug Montgomery, Marty Mathews, John Blake, Phil Pollicelli, Peggy Blake, Mgr.
and Pam Carney, Mgr.
3rd Row
Scott Wood, Bobby Miller, K.T. Salem, Danny Gimler, Will Kirk, Kyle Norris, Craig Zimmerman, Paul
Schoch, Frank Joum.
4th Row
Head Coach, Ray Kiddy, John Duffis, Fred Comer, Steve Schelhaus, Craig George, Todd Geatz, Dave
Kesler, and Assistant Coach, Al Via.
Not Pictured: Leam Geatz, Eric Claycomb, and Mgr. Teresa Mastrangelo.

The first team coached by Kiddy was at Bishop Walsh High School in 1978. Coach Kiddy is at the far left in row four.

113

Jenna Perkins

Track star Jenna Perkins lines up for the 800 meter run for Bishop Walsh School (1982)

RECORD SEASON-Bishop Walsh varsity soccer team recently finished its season with a record 12-4-1. In addition, the Spartans won the Bi-State and City championships with 11-0 and 4-0 records, respectively. Pictured, left to right, are Row 1: Marla DiPasqua, Erin Slonaker, Amy Geatz, Kara Sticher, Andrea Wells, Jill Reinhard, Julie Struntz Row 2: Ted Higson, Craig Spicer, Kenny Miller, Brian Bloom, Mark Amoruso, Mike Bertaux Row 3: Mike Schoch, Craig Gillum, Dick King, Mike Goodfellow, Jim Struntz, Von Fagan, Raul Felipa, Art Zais Row 4: John Mertz, Jason Malak, Kevin Dorsey, Jim Grooms, Ryan Thomas, Keith Silva, Galen Corney Row 5: Alex Fergus, Asst. Coach Tim Rowan, Asst. Coach Joe Rowan, Coach Kiddy, Asst. Caoch Mike Nolan, Asst. Coach Raul Felipa, Matt Pesta

One of the championship seasons for the Bishop Walsh boys' soccer teams (1983)

Ray Kiddy Honored

Ray Kiddy (center), who has stepped down as the Bishop Walsh High soccer coach after guiding the Spartans to a 12-3-1 record and the City and Bi-State League titles, was honored with a dinner recently at the Cumberland Hall of Fame. Shown presenting Kiddy with a present from the team are co-captains Dick King (left) and Craig Gillum (right). Kiddy, a former Valley High and Allegany Community College player, coached the Spartans to three City and three Bi-State League title in his six years as head coach. He will be succeeded by Tim Rowan as the BW coach.

Ray is honored at the Cumberland Hall of Fame after stepping down as soccer coach in 1985.

115

Coach Kiddy (center) with his mother Maxine and father Faye on Ray's wedding day.

Ray and Lori (Richmond) Kiddy on their wedding day (June 1, 1985).

Ray and Lori and their three sons Ross, Garrett, and Gabe in the early years.

Ray with Michelle Barrett on a cold day at Western Maryland College when Michelle won the Maryland 2A Girl's State Cross Country Championship for Allegany High School (1991).

Beall Varsity

Row 1: Joel Greig, Neil O'Driscoll, Jared Lancaster, Darren Johnson, Cass Martin, Jeremy Kneriem, Andy Watkins, and Jason Kirby.

Row 2: Eugene Rice, Lee Ajang, Jared Smith, Brandon Stevens, Jeff Pressman, Corey Delaney, Greg Russ, Jason "Spanky" Robison, and Josh Michaels.

Row 3: Avalon LeDong, Bob Smith, Steve Growden, Brady Greig, Travis Jackson, Justin Weimer, Raphael Baumgartel, Jake Landis and Ray Kiddy.

Beall High School boys' soccer undefeated season (2000).

The Beall High boys' soccer coaching staff following their undefeated season in 2000. Left to right, Dave Blank, Ray, Harry Youngblood, and Avalon LeDong.

Ray completes his NSCAA National Soccer Coaching Diploma at age fifty. Ray is standing in the back row second from right (Bloomsburg University).

Ray's first Potomac State College Men's soccer team in 2010. His son Ross (back row left) and Brad Burr (back row right) were the assistant coaches.

Potomac State College following a home victory in 2011.

Potomac State College Men's Soccer team ranked 8th in the JUCO Division III National Rankings (2012).

Potomac State College Men's Soccer Team ranked 6th in JUCO Division III National Rankings (2013). All American Alec Sproule (back row far right in red keeper jersey). All American Brandon Lee (third from right in back row). Academic All American Jaco

Ray and Lori's sons all earn Eagle Scout standing in Boy Scouts of America.

Ray was still kicking the ball around in the over 52 men's soccer championship in Pittsburgh, Pennsylvania at age 58. Ray is kneeling on the far right when they won that championship.

Ray and Lori are retired and live near Rehoboth Beach, Delaware.

Ray and Lori are grateful for the Rehoboth Beach Running Company and Jack Vassalotti.

Chapter 14: Another Opportunity

"If opportunity doesn't knock, build a door."

-Milton Berle

I always tried to put myself in a good position for growth. The timing and circumstances are so important to weigh.

We need decent people in politics and government.

Life is a game of runs just like the games we compete in.

Just as you are getting started in life, winter arrives.

Overload, be careful not to take on too much of a load.

Always strive to be a team player.

Honor thy mother and father.

A first- year coach has his or her back against the wall-earning players, parents, teachers and administrator's respect.

Following that great 1990 fall soccer season at Frostburg State I focused on being a dad and better husband. Just plain being around was needed. I was loving my job as Director of Recreation and Parks for the City of Frostburg. My bosses were Mayor John Roland and City Administrator Dr. Michael Monahan. Mayor Roland was an English teacher at Allegany High School and Dr. Monahan was a Bishop Walsh

School graduate. They were both top notch people and made the transition back to the area very easy. They were the kind of people that you could easily talk to and know they were proud of their community. John and Mike were the decent type of people that we need in politics and government.

I continued working through the winter as assistant soccer coach for Coach Hegeman at FSU. We hosted our own college indoor soccer tournament and I aided in any way with the development of the team and fundraising. Yes, this included pushing hoagies at our indoor tournament. When working at the college level you have to be a coach, fundraiser, recruiter and do all that is asked of you. I felt part of a team at FSU and was proud to do whatever it would take to assist the cause.

Lori and I were enjoying being parents for the first time and bought land to build a house in the spring of 1990. Our lives were moving in the right direction and we were starting to settle into the City of Frostburg. *We totally enjoyed having our parents close by. As I write, I think about how quickly those times flew by. Ross is now 35 and I am 68. Life is a game of runs just like the games we compete in. Just as you get started, life pushes you through to the final quarter of life.*

I was working, being dad and trying to be the best husband I could be! My phone rang in my office and the Allegany County Public Schools (ACPS) Human Resource office called in early July and wanted me to interview for a physical education teaching position. I had applied back when we were in Baltimore, over a year and half ago. I assumed they were not interested and I had moved on. It turned out they had three PE positions available so I interviewed. I received a letter in early August that I did not get a job with ACPS. It was no big deal. I was happy where I was and what we were doing as a family.

A week passed and the HR director at ACPS called and said, "We have a job for you and we will be back in touch soon." That's all the HR director said before he hung up. I didn't get a word in and it was like some type of a mob call. Now, what do I do? Accept or not! Let my City of Frostburg employees know? Or was this one of my friends just playing a joke on me. I decided to do nothing! I didn't even punt.

A week later the HR director called me and said I had been hired to teach elementary physical education at Cresaptown Elementary school and coach cross country and girls' basketball at Allegany High School. I was excited when they said I would coach two sports, so I accepted and the next stage of my journey began. I immediately went to Mike Monahan, my boss at the City of Frostburg, and let him know my plans. He was disappointed to lose me but totally understood because it was close to a ten-thousand dollars-a-year pay raise. Next, I called Jay Hegeman and gave him the news that I would be coaching cross country at Allegany High School and could not be his assistant soccer coach. Jay was excited for me and wished me well.

Four Jobs

The next day Mike Monahan and I were discussing my departure and he asked if I would like to stay on part time in my recreation and parks position along with all I was going to do in the ACPS system. We worked out the bugs and they offered me half of my salary with the City of Frostburg! I was excited about the money I was going to make for our family but concerned about the workload. What a difference forty- eight hours can make in a person's life. Basically, I had four jobs now. Oh boy! Even if you are a part time coach, if you do it well, it becomes at least twenty hours a week. I don't even remember Lori's thoughts because I was so excited to be a head coach again.

I started coaching cross-country at Allegany on August 15, 1992 and began preparing to teach elementary physical education. I started to wind down the summer for Recreation and Parks and started planning for fall sports and activities for the City of Frostburg.

My cross country team had some good runners. Michelle Barrett led the girls' side that only had four participants. We could not even score in meets until we found that fifth runner. The boys were led by Todd Buckbee and we had good numbers on the boys' side. Michelle had a personal trainer who trained her for cross country. I was good with this and asked her to stretch, do speed work and cool down with the team. She had finished fourth in the state her freshman year, third in the state the next, and last year finished second in the state. Her senior year was her year to win the whole shooting match. This was my best coaching job ever! I stayed out of the way of Michelle and her personal trainer. Michelle had run every day, at least five miles, for the past four years. She only would take Christmas day off, yes four days of rest in four years. It seemed a bit much but as I said I stayed out of the way. Her training proved her success.

Both teams worked hard and we had some success on the boys' side. The girls struggled because we did not have that fifth runner. We had number one each race and Jenna Jordan a good runner, always was helping our count. We just could not be scored with just four runners.

Three of our runners qualified for the Maryland State 2A Meet to be held at Western Maryland College. It has now been renamed William McDaniel College after the schools first college president. See how they did that with initials WMC to save money.

State Championship-Let's Take a Truck

My principal at Allegany High School called me to congratulate us on a successful cross-country season. He also called to inform me that he could put the athletes in a hotel for the night before the meet but did not have money for food or transportation. He asked me what vehicle I drove. I had a Chevy pickup with a cap. He asked me if the student athletes could climb in the back of my pickup and bring their own food. I thought. "You have got to be kidding me." But instead, I said if the ACPS and the parents are good with it then so am I. I am a new employee and always wanted to be a team player.

Later that day the Fort Hill High School cross country coach called me and said he heard we were going to States in a pickup truck and could his two qualifiers ride with us. Oh, what the hell. All parties agreed and off we went with five athletes in the back of my pickup, with food and sleeping bags for comfort. Friday evening, the FH coach and I sat up front and off we went for the State Meet that would start at 9:00 am. I made several stops for an overall wellness check and to make sure no athlete fell to fumes from the truck. We had precious cargo and a potential Maryland State Champion on board. What could go wrong with this scenario? WMC was just two hours and 122 miles from Cumberland, Maryland.

We made it safely, settled into the hotel and had a good night's rest. The girls ran first and Michelle went out and won herself an Allegany High School and Maryland State 2A Championship. What an accomplishment over a four-year high school career and with poor transportation to the meet. The boys did well but no cigar. Good thing – no smoking in the back of truck.

We drove home and had a great weekend. On the way home I saw a hitchhiker. My dad was always kind to hitchhikers and homeless people. He would buy a homeless person in our town a bucket of Kentucky Fried Chicken every time he went for his own order. He also would pick up any hitchhiker, any, even if he was standing on the side of the road with a chainsaw. You guessed it, I picked up the hitchhiker in Frederick, Maryland and put him up front between me and the FH coach. The athletes in the back were laughing their heads off. I wanted to honor my dad anytime I could and I thought with our transportation situation, what the hell.

We pulled off the entire weekend on a skimpy budget - five athletes, two coaches and one hitchhiker. We let him off as requested in Hagerstown, Maryland. No harm, no foul. Probably would not go over so well today! Michelle Barrett was finally a State Champion in cross-country State of Maryland 2A. Michelle went on to get a full ride to Virginia Polytechnic Institute and State University (Virginia Tech) to run cross-country, indoor and outdoor track.

With a solid cross-country track season, my start of elementary teaching, continuing to direct the recreation and parks department and being dad and a husband, the beat went on. I enrolled for the first weekend in November at Penn State University in their women's basketball coaching clinic. The camp was run by the Nittany Lion women's head coach, Rene Portland.

The three-day clinic gave me an excellent refresher in basketball. We started the Allegany High School Camper basketball practice the following Monday. The girls' team was first organized in 1918 and had somewhat of a hot and cold tradition. Coaches came and went and so did great girls' basketball players. But I knew at the first practice this was going to be a great basketball team. The team had height, good ball handlers, speed, and a Division 1 college athlete in Michelle Barrett. Yes, what a treat to coach Michelle in back-to-back sport seasons. We also had speed and good size in rebounding. Some of our headline players were Amy Beeman, Michelle Barrett, Donita Emerson, Monica Fields, Jenni Twigg, Rebecca Wagoner, and Tonya Wharton,

We opened the season in a tournament at Bedford High School about 30 miles north in Bedford Pennsylvania. We started off with a victory over Tyrone High School in a tight game. The next night we beat host Bedford in a runaway and Tonya Wharton was name tournament MVP and Michelle Barrett was name to the All-Tournament team along with Tonya. We were off and running. I felt confident after the Pennsylvania Tournament. Pennsylvania has been a great youth sport development state for many decades. They just plain do it right.

Not Dawn Sloan

Our next game was home against Westmar High School. Westmar was from my hometown in Lonaconing, Maryland. The school's name was changed from Valley to Westmar in 1989 with the consolidation of Valley and Bruce High Schools. The Westmar team was led by a hot-shooting senior Dawn Sloan. Dawn had already signed a full basketball scholarship to the University of Maryland. Not only was this my hometown, but Dawn's father was one of my best friends. I was so proud of Dawn's high school career.

We upset the Westmar team that day by two points only to lose to them at Westmar in the last game of the season by double digits. That last game against Westmar assured both Allegany and Westmar a tie for the Western Maryland Interscholastic Athletic (WMIL) Championship. That last game against Westmar, we worked hard to get to a tie only to have Dawn hit a half court three point shot to take the lead at half by one point. When I went into the locker room, we were deflated by that shot. Westmar dominated the second half. A player like Dawn Sloan can turn a game around with one shot, one steal, and/or one assist. Westmar, with Dawn Sloan went on to win a Maryland State 1A Girls Basketball Championship that year. Dawn Sloan had a good college career although she was sidelined with injuries at the University of Maryland.

We went on at Allegany to lose in the Maryland Class 2A Semi-final to Glenelg High School. We finished the season with a solid 18-6 record. Three of our six loses were to Westmar and two to Bishop McCourt out of Pennsylvania, who also won a state championship that season. The girls at Allegany worked hard in 1991 and they earned my respect by the way they handled having a new coach. *A first- year coach has his or her back against a wall earning players, parents, teachers, and administration respect. Never an easy position to be in.* The girls at Allegany that season made it easier than it should have been. Thank you!!!

Chapter 15: Well, Why Would You Stay?

"If you are going through hell, keep going. Why would you stop in hell?"

-Steve Harvey

When things go wrong, you cannot panic. Take a deep breath and evaluate the situation. How can I turn this into a win?

History may not be kind to you!

Parents should teach respect and remember their children are watching their example.

Parenting is challenging fun, enjoy the ride.

Following the successful Allegany girls' basketball season of 1991-92, I was reading Portrait of an American High School. This book was an Allegany High School Oral History written by the Historical Research Methods Class offered at the school. They wrote that by 1984, girls' basketball had become popular enough to require a junior varsity team. They also wrote that the girls posted mediocre records until Scott Bauer became the coach in 1995. I do not consider that the 1991-92 girls basketball team was a mediocre team having won a share of the Western Maryland Interscholastic League, City Champs and posted a 18-6 record. The hard-working Campers should be offended by this remark, "a mediocre." You can make your mark in history but sometimes it can be overlooked. Research Methods Class got that one wrong. Students in practice!

One Spring afternoon, I was teaching elementary Physical Education at Cresaptown School when Bruce May, the principal of Fort Hill High School, came in, between my classes, to talk to me. Mr. May was a well-known principal and a good athlete back in his day at Hyndman High School in Pennsylvania. He told me that he had a soccer coaching opening for boys next fall and a girls' basketball opening in the winter. He said he knew I loved the game of soccer and also thought that the girls' basketball job at Fort Hill would be a good fit for me following my success at cross town rival Allegany this past season. He also said that within two years he would have a PE opening at the school and I would also be a good fit for that position.

Mr. May also said he had an active athletic booster group that could supply anything I needed. "Hell, we can buy you a dozen soccer balls if you need them." If that was in college and in your budget, it would be cut immediately and money for twelve soccer balls would be moved to some major men's sport. Not a game changer for me! I told Mr. May I would have to discuss this with my wife.

Lori and I were focusing on our new home and Ross. We both agreed that the possibility of coaching and teaching in the same school was a good move for me. We also agreed that the recreation and parks position was going to have to end because it was taking up a lot of my summers

138

and that time was going to be dedicated to be dad to Ross while Lori returned to work as a pharmacist.

I made all parties aware of the change after I let Mr. May know of my decision to move my coaching to Fort Hill High School. I would continue teaching at Cresaptown Elementary School. I loved Cresaptown School students, community, teaching staff and administration. *The parents of Cresaptown School taught respect and they respected all because they knew their children were watching.*

When school ended in June, I began planning for coaching the next fall at Fort Hill. But first I must take care of Ross all summer without Lori's help during the day. It was a challenge—I was a new dad, raising a two-year-old on my own, without his mom. This was work I had never attempted by myself. I loved being with Ross and watching the changes in him each day. I also must admit that around 6:20pm I started peeking out behind the curtain looking for Lori. The hardest and most rewarding work I have ever encountered was during those summers alone with Ross.

August 15, 1992, I began soccer practice at Fort Hill High School. Twenty-two players came out for the varsity squad and twenty-two junior varsity players. Brad Burr who was head of the soccer boosters became my assistant coach and is a good friend to this day. Brad's full-time position was Regional Director for Boy Scouts of America. He was a class act and great with kids. When I selected an assistant I always wanted someone who could take over for me. Lately, with my recent track

139

record, this selection was very important. This selection was also important because we were awaiting the birth of our second child, sometime in September. Pat Nolan, my best friend and best man in my wedding was my second assistant. Pat had a good insight into our players and was great with the finer details like throw in and other specialties. All three of us had a great working relationship.

We started out slowly that fall season. I could see the players were buying into our process and that success would come soon. We were led by Mike Waltz, an outstanding forward who was always around the ball. We started out with a 2-5 record. This had not been a successful squad in the past so this was acceptable to everyone but me. I talked to the team, telling them to keep working hard, to pay attention to details and things will change. We ended up winning the last three of the last five games to finish 5-7. Some of our headline players with Waltz were Tom Barger, Daryl Martin, Steve Barger, and T.J. Smith. We did not qualify for the playoffs after the slow start but our finish gave us a lot to look forward to next fall. That one win away from finishing a 500 season is so close.

Another Son!

Garrett Richmond Kiddy was born on September 28, 1992. This was right around the time we started winning soccer games at Fort Hill. My life was complete with our family, coaching and teaching all falling into place. *As a parent and a coach, you always have to keep all parts of your life in perspective. Don't worry, if you do not, you will recognize your weakness right away.*

140

Winter came quickly when you are burning the candle at both ends as dad, husband and coach. The girls' basketball team at Fort Hill had eleven players. They were hard working girls. The athletes at Fort Hill High School appeared to have a "don't quit" attitude and toughness that I had never seen before. I felt blessed to be coaching at Fort Hill. I knew it then and I still appreciate the Sentinel grit and toughness. My assistant coach for the varsity that winter was Charles 'Buck' Smith, a principal at Washington Middle School and a father of six children. Washington was our feeder school and Buck gave me great insight to our athletes. He also had two children who played for me, Christa in basketball and TJ in soccer.

We fought through a tough season with a slow start. Like soccer, we fought through it and could see the change coming. I measure and never justify success with just winning, however, it is important when you are trying to turn a program around. The record is sometimes all that is remembered the following year. We were led by Carrie Beeman, Gina Brown, Dawn Lancaster, Christa Smith and sharp shooting Renee Shelton. Debbie Jo York provided us with our big inside play. We finished the season 12-10. A highlight of the season was Lori's support and watching her in a large gym carrying Garrett around and chasing Ross during games. It warmed my heart. Once again I knew I had made a great choice in Lori.

During the spring of 1994 Karen Bundy, the Supervisor of Athletic and Physical Education for ACPS, called me and told me to pack up my belongings because a gentleman retired at Fort Hill and the principal wanted me to take his place. I was excited. Bruce May was following through on his promise of a teaching position where I would be coaching two sports. Hurray!

About three months later I received a letter in the mail from Karen Bundy stating I would remain a teacher at Creasaptown School. A teacher at Washington Middle School was coaching football at Fort Hill. He was a math teacher but had a certification in Physical Education and the Athletic Director/ Football Coach Mike Calhoun wanted him instead of me. What football coach wants a soccer coach in the school teaching. None, none. That's right, none. Karen Bundy could not call or come see me but wrote me a letter! This was also very disappointing. Fortunately , I liked my teaching job at Creasaptown School and coaching at Fort Hill. I will be patient! Promises are just that, unless you have them in writing!

That summer I was home with Ross and Garrett. Now I had double work at home. I had given up the Frostburg Recreation and Parks Director part-time job because I had a full plate for the summer. Being dad, all summer was a great experience but difficult to keep up with all of the household chores. I do not know how a full-time mother does it. I hired a gentleman and his daughter to cut my grass weekly. The daughter was a Fort Hill grad and dad, a Sentinel supporter. It was great to help their family. The summer went by quick and August was around the corner.

We began soccer practice on August 15, 1993. Everyone associated was excited but not any more than I. Prior to the 12 regular season games, we would open the season with a scrimmage tournament with four teams in Altoona, Pennsylvania. The team showed up in pretty good shape following summer workouts. We would run a two-mile run every Saturday morning from Washington Middle School practice field to Willow Brook Road and back. This run required us to take on a tough rolling hill, out and back, 5K. I would win most of the runs being only 36 years of age! Sometimes TJ Smith would beat me. Bucks' son was quite an athlete and determined individual.

We were determined to be the best conditioned team on our schedule. We entered the Altoona Scrimmage tournament with two opening wins and that evening finished with a 0-1 loss to host Altoona High School. Televised on the local television, the game was attended by a nice crowd and this was a great day for us and the team was flying high, finishing the day in Altoona. One player said on the way home, "Coach we are going undefeated." This was an all-day scrimmage tournament and I only had one thing on my mind, getting home to Lori and my boys.

A Turn of Events

The team fought through some tough games, far from the undefeated prediction. Then an unpredicted series of events took place. Someone wrote an anonymous letter to my Supervisor of Athletics, Karen Bundy, that we participated in an illegal tournament in Altoona, Pennsylvania. It was determined that if a scrimmage tournament collected an admission fee and we were on television, we were in violation. Both were Maryland Public School Scholastic Athletic

Association violations and we had to forfeit the entire season and we were not allowed to participate in the playoffs.

Mike Calhoun was my athletic director at Fort Hill and also the head football coach. His teams had suffered a 4-6 season in 1991 and he was starting to turn his program around with back-to-back 10-2 seasons. Mike was supportive of all sports at FH so I went to him to plead our case of the scrimmage violations and ask how we could remedy the situation. He told me that it was a done deal and there was nothing I could do about it. I called Karen Bundy and I said this is my mistake and the student athletes should not be penalized. I asked to see the letter and she declined my request. I told her that we were going to win our last two games and qualify for the playoffs. She said we would not beat Flintstone and that was too bad. Well, she was wrong. We won the last two games and beat Flintstone to finish 8-3-1 on the season. We were not allowed to be in the State Playoffs and the season was over.

I never felt so responsible for this mistake that affected our Fort Hill soccer athletes and parents. Those boys gave everything thing they had that fall of 1993. I was proud of their effort and so disappointed in the outcome. They deserved better. Karen Bundy took it one step further to ask that I be denied the opportunity to coach soccer in 1994. That decision was overturned. The only satisfaction I received that fall was that I could return as soccer coach in 1994. Fat chance! The pattern continues!

Would Someone Pick Me Up?

I did continue to coach the Fort Hill girls' basketball team that winter. We had a good nucleus back and I was excited to rinse that fall soccer season from my mouth. Our returners were all back and I knew we could make the playoffs. We completed the season with a 12-10 record and finished fourth in our region. I moved Jenna Cessna, a freshman, up to varsity for another big inside player. Jenna was a strong country girl and could move a barn by herself. Only the top four teams qualify for playoffs.

We went into the playoff game with a renewed energy. We could see the girls' program heading in the right direction. We had to play the playoff game at North Hagerstown High School on their home floor. I didn't feel good about playing on their court but, when we arrived, I saw three officials from our region. Well, that was a relief. No hometowner here at North High!

It was the worst officiated game I saw in my brief basketball coaching career. We lost by double digits and I was frustrated. I went into the official locker room and told all three officials that was the worst officiated game I had ever witnessed. This was in the "Dan Hurley" sense at UConn. They kept their silence and I could tell , in their eyes, they could not believe their ears. I walked out and slammed the door.

This concluded my coaching career at Fort Hill High School as I continued my frustration with the school and the administration. I resigned the following Monday. Nothing fell in place the way I thought, was told, or dreamed about at Fort Hill High School. Fort Hill is still number one in my book despite the outcome. Great student athletes who worked hard to see the job completed. That is all you can ask as a coach of your athletes. A job well done by the Fort Hill athletes.

Chapter 16: Keep Your Feet Moving

"Passion first and everything will fall into place."

-Holly Holm

The difference between coaching women and men is simple. Women never want to see the game video. They admit they made a mistake and never want to watch the mistake again. Men are the exact opposite. They will watch it three times and still make an excuse for why it happened.

Assistant coaches should be eager to learn and take initiative in their position.
Praise, praise, praise your children.
As a coach, be a good steward of your program.
Do not deceive a player about their abilities and how they will fit into the team.
Every player must pull their own weight. The broom handle must fit everyone's hand.

In February 1994, Dr. Constance McGovern, Provost and Vice President for Academic Affairs at Frostburg State University, announced my hiring as the first women's soccer coach in FSU history. At this point, my overall coaching record stood at 96-84-4. Not too shabby, considering the struggles some of my teams endured. When you keep starting over with a new program, you never gain the momentum needed to build stability and rack up wins. Stability is necessary for a coach's confidence. However, I was never afraid to take on a new challenge.

Loyal Park was the Athletic Director at FSU, and he was very supportive of our women's soccer program. He also led the drive to start women's volleyball that same fall. Many of the instructors I had at FSU as an undergrad and master's program student were still there, and they made me feel at home. Jay Hegeman was still coaching the men's soccer team, and he was a great resource.

I realized that, as a new intercollegiate program at FSU, we were not starting from the grassroots since we had been playing soccer as a club sport for the past three seasons. I believed back then that with three recruiting seasons, we would be able to compete at the regional level of the NCAA. I just didn't expect the immediate success.

Ron Ploude, Darcy Legoy, and Alan Green were my assistant coaches for that inaugural season at FSU. They were graduate assistants in the physical education department and wanted to get their feet wet in coaching. They gave great insight to our ladies with their varied backgrounds in athletics. They were eager to learn and took initiative in organizing our first women's team.

Ron Ploude has served as a successful baseball coach at Skidmore College since 1998. He has led Skidmore to seven twenty-plus win seasons. His Thoroughbreds have won league titles in 2012, 2010, 2007, 2005, and 1999. Ron has been named Liberty League Coach of the Year four times and ECAC Coach of the Year in 2010.

We started in the fall of 1994 with our first women's varsity soccer team ever. We began in August with full support from the university—in budget, recruiting through enrollment services, and a strong athletic program that provided good facilities and a strong schedule. Dina Lastner played up front, supported by some strong midfield and defensive players. We completed that first season 9-7-1. It was a respectable start, and we were in every game.

Community

While continuing to teach elementary physical education at Cresaptown School, I wanted to progress both in the school and in the community. I was able to get the school involved in the Jump Rope for Heart program, run by the American Heart Association, and the "Kids, I Did It! Run," promoted by *Runner's World* magazine.

The Jump Rope for Heart program involved students at Cresaptown School raising money for the American Heart Association. At different fundraising levels, students could earn various prizes along with a T-shirt. The school was given 30 jump ropes as a reward for our participation. I used the jump ropes for a two-minute warm-up for each class. The kids loved the program, which concluded with end-of-year jump rope games and after-school activities. We played music selected by the students and incorporated jump rope exercises. Our parents at Cresaptown were very supportive of the program.

After four years, we had raised over forty thousand dollars for the American Heart Association. When we reached the forty-thousand-dollar level, I was invited to an evening dinner in Baltimore sponsored by the American Heart Association. This meant a lot to me, since my dad had two brothers and a sister who died of heart disease. They were all in their forties when they passed. My own father died of congestive heart failure at age 71 on January 22, 2002.

In the fall of 1994, FSU was searching for a women's softball coach to begin a new program. Like women's soccer, they had previously sponsored a club women's softball team. I stepped up and called Loyal Park, our athletic director, and said that if he was in a pinch, I would coach the women's softball team for the spring of 1995. Loyal was excited and said the job was mine: "Thank you, Ray." I would begin recruiting and coaching the team as soon as the 1994 fall season was complete. I didn't need another job, but I stepped up because coaching is like a disease, and for some reason, I did not want to go into remission.

I was now an elementary PE teacher and coach of two college women's sports at the NCAA Division III level. I remember being announced in *USA Today* newspaper as the coach of both sports. For me, this seemed like big time and a long way from the Avenue Pissant backyard football I coached when I was ten years old. Coaching and teaching were my passions, and I was excited to be leading teams at my alma mater, FSU.

Runner's World magazine sponsored a "Kids, I Did It! Run" program. It involved students signing up and training to run one mile or 100 yards, based on age groupings. We held the program on a spring day at Allegany

Community College. Each student received a T-shirt and participated in stretching before their race.

Following the run, we provided fruit and drinks for all participants. The "Kids, I Did It! Run" drew over two hundred participants in its first year, and I organized it for four years. The Allegany County Health Department became involved and donated six hundred dollars each year to help us create a great afternoon for our young runners. Once again, the Cresaptown community was very involved in the program. They were always supportive of the school and our activities.

Praise, praise, praise your children.

Two New Arrivals!

My second season at FSU began on a high note. Gabriel Charles Kiddy, my third son, was born on August 15, 1995. We were all excited for the arrival of Gabe, but no one more than Ross and Garrett. Oh, what fun three boys will have!

My first talented recruit was Danielle Picker, a scoring machine out of North Carroll High School. Danielle had good speed, but even better skills. She was a team player and distributed the ball well, and we would be able to build a successful team around our freshman.

Salisbury State University was our in-state rival. They had started their women's soccer program the same year we did, in 1994. We lost 0-3 to them in our first season, but closed the gap in 1994, losing 1–2 in overtime. Salisbury was coached by a professional recruiter in college

151

sports, Jim Berkman. His soccer teams were loaded with great recruits, and he was a steady coach. He was a full-time coach, and I was part-time. I felt good about the gap we had closed. We finished the season 10–7–1 in 1994—one more win than the year before, but we were a more competitive team.

Jim Berkman only coached women's soccer at Salisbury University for a few years. His passion and expertise were in men's lacrosse. Jim has been the Salisbury lacrosse coach for over 36 years, winning 620 matches with only 63 losses. Incredible statistics, especially when you add in the outstanding run of 13 National Championships in NCAA Division III.

Indoor Softball?

The first women's varsity softball team began in January 1995. We had a good nucleus from the club team the season prior to our varsity inaugural season. A few freshmen were newcomers, but I really did not have a good handle on recruiting college softball players. The women's team was excited about being part of the first varsity softball squad.

We had several strong players returning from the club team. They were second baseman Jill Baker, first baseman Sonja Peterson, top pitcher Jessica Paugh, and catcher Steph Walker. Walker was our best all-around athlete and was above the level of NCAA Division III. Scottie Showalter gave us a strong backup pitcher.

Winters in Frostburg, Maryland, can be brutal, and this winter was no different. We had an auxiliary area in the downstairs of the Dr. Harold

Cordts Center on campus for practice space. This auxiliary area had batting cages and was a good-size space. Prior to our first game of the season, we spent three practices outside in a snow-plowed parking lot.

Our first scheduled game was a trip for a doubleheader at Bridgewater College. This was during our spring break. Bridgewater College in Bridgewater, Virginia, was a three-hour bus trip, and I was the head coach and the bus driver. If you drove your own bus, you saved one hundred dollars in your budget. Being a new program, I thought we would need every dollar. The university gave me a great budget because they wanted the women to have a successful start. I also wanted to be a good steward of the first women's softball program.

We arrived at Bridgewater College for a doubleheader, where they had just experienced two hours of hard rain prior to our games. Their head coach said, "We obviously can't play outside today, but we have an old field house that's been replaced by a new one. We don't care if we beat the old one up because it will be demolished in the near future. If you' want to play indoors, the field would be 100 feet down the first base line and 200 feet down the third base line. If the ball hits the ceiling, we'll call it a dead ball."

I thought about the setup and knew my ladies were anxious to start the season. I agreed, and it took three hours to complete the first game ever for the FSU varsity squad. There were a lot of runs scored, and we lost that first game indoors, but we had fun, and I loved the enthusiasm of our team.

I remember that first women's team as hard-working and very supportive of me, my coaching staff, and their fellow teammates. Steph Walker was our starting catcher, and she had so much energy. She would back up the throw at first base on every hit to the infield. That's hustle and determination! You remember an athlete like Steph.

They cheered for each other enthusiastically in the dugout. They rattled the dugout cage. They had all the cheers down, like "Rally on two! Red hot—action, action, we want action!" and so on.

I remember going to Bethany College in West Virginia when they were undefeated at 14–0. We beat them in the first game of the doubleheader. Before the second game, I went up to the umpires at home plate and overheard their catcher say to a teammate, "We're not going to lose to a bunch of cheerleaders again." We had them rattled, and we swept the doubleheader. That was a great mark for our first season.

We finished the season 16–14, and we were all proud of that record. It was difficult to finish above .500, but we all scratched and clawed like true Bobcats. It was a tough season for me personally—three sons at home, back-to-back college-level seasons, and recruiting for two college teams.

The recruiting part was becoming easier for me. I wanted the players to know that I wanted them to be successful as individuals and as a team—on the field, and more importantly, in the classroom. Everyone who is part of a team has a commitment and a responsibility. Everyone has a role.

154

No one plays the role of permanent benchwarmer on my teams. If a player can't contribute on the field, I won't lead her on or keep her on the team. I would never deceive a player about her abilities. It wouldn't be fair.

The broomstick handle had to fit every player's hand as well. We all had to pull our own weight with equipment, setup, and taking care of each other as good teammates. As a coach, you have to be a good role model. Practice what you preach.

Lori had been taking a break from work. She was either not working or working part-time over the past two seasons while I focused on PE and coaching. Coaching two college teams had helped us financially. It helped fill the gap left by Lori staying home. It was nothing compared to Lori's pharmacy salary, but as a family, you do whatever you can to make ends meet. It's part of the American dream—being able to make choices because of our freedom.

The 1996 season was going to be our best at FSU for women's soccer. I had three years of recruiting under my belt, and those who had played were progressing each year. We used the winter season to play indoors at FSU. Our only available time slot in the gymnasium was 10:00–11:00 p.m. because of in-season sports. We played two nights a week following my softball practices and traveled to some local colleges to compete in tournaments at West Virginia University and indoor facilities in Pennsylvania.

The 1996 team was solid at all positions, and we were competing in the preliminary conference called the Allegheny Mountain Collegiate

Conference (AMCC). The AMCC would have its inaugural season in 1997 but ran a trial schedule in 1996. We were also excited to be part of a soccer conference. The new conference would consist of Chatham, Frostburg, Lake Erie, La Roche, Medaille, Pitt–Greensburg, Penn State–Altoona, and Penn State–Behrend.

We competed well in the conference that preliminary season, as well as with our regular schools such as Bethany, Cabrini, Hood, Salisbury, and Villa Julie. We were traveling from Pittsburgh to Philadelphia, and it was taking its toll on me as a part-time coach driving the bus to away games. Some nights I would get back at 1:30 a.m. following a game, dinner, and the drive home—only to be back at my PE job by 7:30 a.m. for elementary bus duty. I also remember waking up at 2:30 a.m. some mornings and going to FSU to do paperwork for meal money, bus or van orders, or just to plan a practice or game strategy.

Can We Play with a Division I Program?

Another highlight of 1996 was that we scheduled a match against Division I Naval Academy. They were coached by United States Women's National Soccer Team member Carin Gabarra, who had also played at the University of California, Santa Barbara.

Here we were, a NCAA Division III soccer program in our third season, and the Naval Academy wanted to play us. I figured they needed a tune-up game, but I thought, why not? I had a habit of playing anyone who would be an exciting challenge for our team and help put us on the map.

Carin Gabarra called me the week before our game to tell me they would arrive in Frostburg the Sunday prior to our Monday game. She wanted to know if they could practice on our game field that Sunday evening. I said yes immediately because they were willing to come to our place to play the game, so I wanted to cooperate.

Plus, I thought, while they were practicing, I would go to the third floor of our library and watch their practice. Not to gain secretive information, but to see how she ran a pre-game practice. I know what you're thinking: surely you didn't watch for game info for the next day like some Michigan football coach in the sign-stealing scandal back in 2023. Okay, maybe I wanted to see their personnel in action.

We lost to the Naval Academy 1-5 the next day. Carin Gabarra's storied coaching career continues, as --she remains the Naval Academy Head Women's Coach in 2025. She first took the position in 1993.

We finished the 1996 season 12–5–1. Our first three seasons at FSU produced a record of 31–19–3. I felt pretty good about our three-year progress. The next three coaches at FSU women's soccer had records as follows: Courtney McClelland, 25–12; Carrie Lysik, 39–22; and Brian Parker, 40–13–7. The only difference was that I was the only part-time coach, while the others were full-time employees at FSU.

Following the 1996 soccer season, Loyal Park, our AD at Frostburg, called me in for a meeting. He offered me a full-time position coaching soccer and softball. The only catch was that it was not a benefit-eligible position. Loyal offered to pay for my family health insurance the first year until it became eligible.

I knew other employees at FSU who had waited years for their positions to become benefit-eligible. I already had a good teaching position in Allegany County Public Schools with benefits and a retirement package. Lori and I discussed the offer but thought it was too risky.

I was always appreciative of Loyal having the confidence in me as a college coach and often wondered what would have happened if I had taken his offer. I guess I was destined to be a part-timer for a long time.

Thank God for a Near Miss

I started the women's softball winter practices in 1997. Lori had gone back to work full-time, and I had to pick up my oldest son, Ross, from school and take him to softball practice with me. He loved it as he sat in our auxiliary practice gym doing his homework. Ross was seven years old, and he loved the attention from the girls on the team, and they loved having him around.

In the second week of winter practice, Ross got up from his homework and walked right into the path of a girl taking a practice swing. She fortunately missed his head by inches. If she had made contact with his head, it could have been devastating, if not deadly, for Ross.

As I watched this incident, which was completely Ross's fault, or more importantly, his dad's fault, I thought, *He's only seven years old, and I'm putting him in a dangerous situation.*

When I arrived home that evening, I told Lori about the incident and said we needed to come up with another plan. The other plan came down to me giving up the FSU women's softball coaching job. It was early enough in the winter season for my assistants to take over, and I left both FSU women's coaching positions. It was a tough decision, but the right one for my family. Family always comes second, right after God.

I had a bachelor's, two master's degrees, and had a wonderful experience in the four years I coached at FSU. I love that school and owe many thanks to the student-athletes and employees of Frostburg State University.

Chapter 17: Allegany Again

"When life gives you lemons, make lemonade."

-Elbert Hubbard

You can go back home! Just reconnect and have fun. Cherish the past memories and the new beginnings.
Most things in life are out of your control.
You never know how your players see you. Remember: they are watching your every move.

After my exit from Frostburg State University coaching, I was satisfied to be a dad and teach PE at Cresaptown School. As I settled into that feeling of not coaching, I saw that Allegany High School was looking for a boys' head soccer coach. Their current coach was Rodney Lehman. Yes, the *Rodney Lehman* that broke our hearts when I was at Bishop Walsh coaching the boys. He scored two goals to upset BW in 1984. Rodney was leaving Allegany High School to take a full-time PE and coaching position in the state of Ohio.

I loved my coaching stint in 1991 with cross country and girls' basketball at Allegany High School. I immediately called Roger Flanagan, the principal at Allegany, and he basically offered me the job during that one phone call. He later told me he was so excited I called and wanted the position that he felt like *Pele* had just called him and wanted to come to Allegany! So, I threw myself right back into the soccer pit. As I said, coaching was like a disease to me, and I never liked being in remission.

I took the job in July and we started practice in mid-August. I had not followed local soccer recently, since I was coaching the past three years at FSU. Allegany County Public Schools hadn't started girls' soccer yet, so there wasn't much reason for me to follow local soccer in the early '90s. Lord knows I was busier than a snowplow in a blizzard, with a family, teaching, and being a part-time coach. What I was soon to find out was just how good Allegany boys' soccer could be.

History Lesson

Boys' soccer at Allegany High School was first organized in the fall of 1921 by the school's students and parents. Soccer struggled at Allegany because football was the more popular sport. The soccer program ended before World War II, in 1939, and it would take another forty years for the Allegany boys' soccer program to be reborn. In the fall of 1977, Don Amoruso and a group of parents formed Allegany's modern team.

Don Amoruso was a fine soccer coach in the Western Maryland area. He actually grew up on the same street I did in Lonaconing, Maryland. I took over the storied program started by Don Amoruso and his assistant Bill Dean. Don's son, Mark Amoruso, played for me at Bishop Walsh back in the 1980s. I coached against Don, and we became good friends following some good, competitive games back in the day.

My first game at the helm at Allegany was not a memorable start. We were the first Allegany team to lose to Southern Garrett in soccer history, falling 2–3. O'boy! The goalkeeper for that Southern team was Jonathan Price. He later became Southern High School's boys' soccer coach and is now the men's soccer coach at Garrett College in McHenry, Maryland.

The boys were deflated, but I could see the team working hard and coming together. We had some of the most memorable players I ever coached: Joe Bidwell, Jay Litten, Joel Methany, Arnel Kazazic, Andy Sam, Matt Zealand, and Robbie Stansbury in the goal. From that point on, we dedicated ourselves to turning the program around. Over the next 10 games, we went 8-2-1.

We moved on to the playoffs and faced Southern Garrett in our first playoff game. It was a hard-fought battle that saw us avenge our season-opening loss with a 4–3 victory for the Campers. We then hosted our second-round playoff game against Clear Spring and won 3–1. We had now won six of our last seven games, going 7-0-1. We were excited, sitting at a 10-2-1 record after a slow start to 1997. Oh no! Hold on.

On Wednesday of that week, the Supervisor of Athletics called me at Cresaptown School. As I know, this can never be good. He said that due to the predicted rain for Thursday, we would have to move our game to another site, away from our home field at Greenway Avenue Stadium. The reason was that Fort Hill football had a big game Friday night against Martinsburg, West Virginia, and the field needed to be in good shape for that game. Yes, this was still a grass field!

My response: "You have got to be kidding me."

The supervisor replied, "I wish I was."

The supervisor was a former principal at Fort Hill High School. What a pattern of getting the jilt from Fort Hill. We had worked hard all season to scrap and earn a home playoff game, and now we were denied that opportunity.

He said, "You can choose any field in the county to play, and I'll make sure it's lined."

I asked, "What choice do I have?"

He repeated himself and said, "You can play anywhere in Allegany County but not at your home field at Fort Hill High School," which evidently owns and operates Greenway Avenue Stadium. They truly do, but don't. Incidentally, the next year in 1998, Greenway Avenue Stadium added artificial turf. Coinkydink? I think not!

I put up as much of a fight for my boys as I could, short of losing my job. I thought about the situation after I cooled down. The supervisor told me he didn't like being in this position any more than I did. Don't bet on it!

Anyway, Flintstone High School was undefeated in our region. If we could win our next game against Williamsport High School, we'd have to play Flintstone next. So I told the supervisor I wanted to play the Williamsport game *at* Flintstone School.

When I arrived for practice that Wednesday, the boys were pumped. But I had to break the news that our playoff game was being moved due to a regular-season football game. This is the kind of news always handed to the soccer coach to deliver to his/her team and never to the people making the decisions.

Minor sport coaches: be prepared to be the scapegoat. Never fair, and hard to swallow!

The boys understood why I made my decision, and fortunately, by this point in the season, they had confidence in my judgment.

The next day we arrived for our pregame warm-up at Flintstone School. I was met by Bob Rinker, the head coach of Flintstone High School. His team, which was undefeated, could not host their own game due to the record of South Hagerstown High School. They had earned more points based on the size of the schools they had beaten.

Bob said, "Why in the hell would you want to play this playoff game on our field?"

He was right. Flintstone's field was part dirt and part grass and sloped with a 2% grade. One corner flag had an oak tree overhanging it, making corner kicks nearly impossible. Trust me, the Fort Hill football team wouldn't even hold a picnic on that field.

I told Bob, "We're here because next Tuesday we're going to beat your ass on your own field." We needed the practice to get ready for that game. I hoped I got into Bob's head with that comment. He laughed and got on his bus for the South Hagerstown game.

We fought Williamsport in a tough game, and in the end, we were victorious 2–1. We learned that day to stay away from corner kicks at the end under the old oak tree and to keep the ball on the ground, given the short and narrow field. The bench side of the field was also sloped, so the ball wasn't going out of bounds on that side if it stayed on the ground.

We left Flintstone High School that day feeling good about the Williamsport win. We now had three practices to get ready for the Flintstone game next Tuesday, if they won that night.

He's on The Field; He's on The Field!

Flintstone won their playoff game against South Hagerstown 2–0. They would now move on to the West Region final at home against us. Allegany had never won 11 games in school history and had never played in the Maryland State playoffs. However, Flintstone was a storied soccer program and remained unbeaten at 12-0-2, with a 7-0-1 home record that season. One of those ties had been against Allegany just three weeks earlier, a 2–2 match.

We arrived at Flintstone that afternoon feeling pretty well prepared. We had played them in the regular season to a 2–2 tie, and this was now our third game on their home field. My boys were excited about our position. Our fans came out and supported us, and we were pumped.

Ten minutes into the game, their coach Bob Rinker fell onto the field. Remember, I said the bench side of the field was on a slope. I yelled to the official, "He's on the field! He's on the field!" I just wanted to keep our players light during the playoff game. Everyone laughed, including the official. Bob got off the ground, came over to me, and said quietly, "You asshole."

The score at halftime was 0–0. We didn't seem tight as a team when I spoke at halftime. I reminded them that we had never been in this playoff position before as a soccer school, so let's play loose with nothing to lose.

The one thing that bothered me was losing the opening coin flip. They chose to go uphill in the first half, so they would be going down a 2% grade in the second half. We hadn't scored going in that direction during the first half.

We held firm on defense, had a breakaway and scored to go up 1–0 with ten minutes to go in the West Region Final. My parents were at the game, and a friend told me my dad jumped higher than Michael Jordan when we went up 1–0. As suspected, the Flintstone Aggies would be coming over the hill with that downhill grade. They tied the game 1–1 with three minutes to go in regulation.

Penalty Kicks For Money

The game went into two ten-minute overtime periods. It was golden goal, but no one could break the plane to score.

In 1997, a playoff game would be decided by 11 penalty kicks from each team. We had prepared for penalty kicks during the playoffs. At the end of each practice, I had the team take five penalty kicks against each other, rotating our regular keepers through different groupings. With only two goals, we used cones to keep things moving. I thought we had the upper hand on penalty kicks just because we were a more finesse team than Flintstone.

Nope! They won the game before we even got to seven kicks. I told Robby Stansbury, our keeper, to protect the middle of the goal. With eleven kicks, some are going to go down the middle. Flintstone buried their first seven in the corners.

After the game, I congratulated Bob Rinker, the Flintstone coach, and wished him good luck in the final four. I also said I thought we had them when we went to penalty kicks. He said he wasn't worried at that point. He told me he didn't set aside time at practice for penalty kicks. Instead, he said, "I just come to practice ten minutes late each day, and the kids take penalty kicks against each other for quarters." I guess it helps to have money on the line.

We went home that evening disappointed, but I had pride in my team and the way they played the entire season. Flintstone, with a 13-0-2 record, lost the state semifinal game 0–2 to St. Michael High School.

At Christmas time, I received a nice card from Matt Zealand, who had scored eight goals and two assists on the season. Matt was a class act and came from a nice family. His dad was a well-known psychiatrist in our area. Matt included a six-paragraph letter, thanking me for leading the team and writing that I had an outstanding way of communicating with my players.

You never know how the players view you as a coach. You just try to lead, be a student of the game, and pass along everything you've learned over the years to your players.

Chapter 18: Steps to Becoming an Indian

"To educate a man in mind and not in words is to educate a menace to society."

-Theodore Roosevelt

We do not remember our first baby steps. We may have been told about those important steps. In most cases, we needed a take-off chair, encouragement, and most of the time, a helping hand.
Be thankful for our school administrators and teachers. They do their best every day to educate and protect our sons and daughters.
When you take on a new position, beware of sharks.
Strive to learn every day.
Ninety percent of the time, school consolidation is necessary and the right choice.
Life is not always fair, so join the circus!

In February of 1998, it was a typical winter afternoon at Cresaptown School. The principal, Blaine Watson, the custodial staff, and I were setting up chairs in the gymnasium around 2:00 p.m. for a PTA meeting that evening. An intruder entered the gym and started taking off his boots and lacing up his tennis shoes. Blaine asked me if I knew this individual. I said no, so the principal went over to the person to ask if he could help.

The intruder stood up and started doing karate moves, acting in an unusual manner. Blaine told the custodians to lock down the gymnasium.

They locked Blaine, me, and the intruder in the gymnasium. The intruder started picking up metal chairs and throwing them at Blaine and me. Blaine ran toward me and said, "Whatever you do, don't let this guy get hold of you." We dodged chairs for about ten minutes before we got fed up. We started winging chairs back at the intruder.

It took the police about twenty minutes to arrive at the school. Four officers subdued the intruder and took him into custody. Blaine and one police officer suffered hand injuries. Our school was lucky the individual didn't have a weapon that day.

The incident caused alarm throughout the school. The students, staff, and teachers were visibly shaken. Blaine's quick reaction to lock down the gymnasium was the right move. It confined the man to one area where students were not in harm's way. Blaine and I were honored at a school board meeting for doing an excellent job in preventing a situation that could have been a lot worse.

The intruder was found to be an 18-year-old Cresaptown man. He was taken to Sacred Heart Hospital for psychological evaluation. He was charged with disrupting school operations, disorderly conduct, and causing up to $1,000 in damages.

When you least expect it in schools, a situation can unravel quickly. Every school community in the United States must be aware that an emergency situation can happen to you. As I said earlier, we need to be thankful for our administrators and teachers, doing their best every day to educate and protect our sons and daughters.

Following the 1997 season at Allegany High School, rumors started circulating in the building that George Bishields, the legendary soccer coach at Mount Savage, was going to retire at the end of the 1998 school year. I was approached by the supervisor of athletics to consider taking the teaching and soccer coaching position at Mount Savage.

Again, I had always wanted to teach and coach in the same school, just as I did at Bishop Walsh School. If you remember, the first game I ever coached was against Coach Bishields and his Mount Savage Indians back in 1978.

George had become a friend over the course of my early coaching career, and as a soccer coach, I had the utmost respect for him. He had led the Soccer Indians for the past 27 years, winning two Maryland State Championships and compiling a record of 269-81-20. I actually played soccer at Valley High School against Bishields-coached Indian teams. It never turned out well for Valley.

I told the supervisor of athletics that I was interested and would jump at the chance to leave Cresaptown and Allegany to teach and coach at Mount Savage School. It came to fruition, and I packed up my things that spring and moved my teaching/coaching tools to my new school. I had big shoes to fill and knew this was going to be a great challenge!

Coach Bishields had led undefeated teams five years in a row from 1972–1976.

Mike Mathews, a sports writer for the *Cumberland Times-News*, wrote an article about George Bishields and me and the passing of the baton. The article was titled *Kiddy Begins New Job Today, Step by Step*. It gave George his due and noted that while I had built programs before, now "Kiddy has to maintain a program, and that could be a tougher task." Mount Savage had 30-plus concrete steps to climb to reach the soccer field. I knew this was going to be a climb for me as I worked to maintain the soccer tradition with the Indians.

You Might Not Fit in Here

Before the first practice, I drove over to Mount Savage to assist with physicals for fall athletes. I passed a runner on the side of the road and pulled over to ask who he was. I introduced myself, and he said, "My name is Adam Stafford, and I'm going to be your goalkeeper. I'm out running five miles." If your keeper is out running five miles on his own, you've got a dedicated goalkeeper. I shook his hand and told him I looked forward to working with him and the rest of the team.

When I entered the lobby at Mount Savage, I was greeted by another female coach at the school. She said, "Welcome and congratulations. However, you've always coached in Cumberland where there are many talented athletes. Here at Mount Savage, you have to *make* athletes." I took this as a welcome, I think!

As I settled into my office before the start of the season, I made one phone call. I called Coach George Bishields to see if he would like to be my assistant that fall. He kindly thanked me but said, "Ray, you need your space, and I would be a distraction to the team and the community. You need this year to set your own way and guide the team in the direction you want it to go. I wish you luck, and if there are any questions, please don't hesitate to give me a call." George Bishields was always a class act when dealing with friends and fellow coaches.

We were led in 1998 by ten seniors in my first Mount Savage season. Remember my rule: ten or more seniors on a varsity soccer team will put you "in the money." Dave Blank, who had been George's assistant, agreed to stay on as my assistant coach. Dave was from the Mount Savage community and knew all of our junior varsity and varsity players. He was a great resource and gave me, the new guy, a jumpstart.

The Mount Savage soccer players were accustomed to practicing hard for George Bishields, and they continued that effort for me. I was proud of this team that had to make a big transition in head coaches. We were led by Steve Bennett, Chris and Danny Bloskey, Brian DeHaven, Jason Loar, Darren Johnson, Adam Moulden, Larry O'Baker, Jason Skidmore, Dave Sheppard, Joe Shaffer, and Adam Stafford. Brian DeHaven was named Defensive Player of the Year in Western Maryland.

We boasted six shutouts and allowed an average of seven shots per game on defense. The defense gave up just 16 goals in the first 15 games, and only 20 goals over the full 16-game season. We finished as runner-up in both the Western Maryland area and the Western Maryland Interscholastic League. We finished the season 13–3. Those 13 wins were the most for a Mount Savage team since the 1989 state runner-up squad that went 15–1.

That 1998 team was one of the best high school soccer teams I was associated with as a head coach. It also shows the courage that George Bishields had to step down when there was still a great team on the shelf. Most coaches step down when the cupboard is bare. Not George.

Teaching at a K–12 School

That first school year at Mount Savage was a good start for me in teaching. Mount Savage was a K–12 school. A school day would begin with kindergarten in the first period and end with seniors just before soccer practice. I started my days as a nice guy tying wet shoelaces and ended them giving high school seniors stern instructions to close the day.

I decided I would enroll in Frostburg University's Administration and Supervision master's program. I already had my master's in physical education, but I thought that I might someday need a twelve-month position in administration to help my family and earn a higher income. Did I have the time for teaching, coaching, being a good husband, and raising three growing boys? The answer is no, but I always enjoyed setting a new goal and loved a challenge.

I started the A&S program at Frostburg in January of 1999. I enjoyed the challenge of the classes and being back on campus. I would need another 30 graduate credits, which would bring me to 60-plus credits total, boosting my salary as well. A win-win situation. The other perk was that ACPS would reimburse me for tuition if I earned a B or better. Piece of cake. We all have to strive to learn every day.

After graduating 10 seniors in 1998, the 1999 team had only six returning seniors. I knew this would be a challenge. Of more concern, we had only two freshmen on the junior varsity team. Enrollment at Mount Savage School was dwindling, and there was talk of consolidating with Beall High School in Frostburg, Maryland.

George Bishields Returns

Dave Blank, my assistant coach, took over the girls' team at Mount Savage. After Dave moved on, I approached George Bishields again. George's wife had put a bug in my ear and asked me to get George out of the house. I asked George to be my assistant coach, and he jumped at the opportunity. I was so excited to work with the best in the soccer coaching business. We were a good team, and George was such a gentleman to work with.

Each day during the hot preseason, George would ask me, "Do you want iced tea or lemonade tomorrow?" And he would bring it each day for my enjoyment, along with a work ethic that was second to none in coaching.

The 1999 campaign was an exciting season. We finished the season 10–5. Joe Shaffer, Adam Moulden, and Larry O'Baker led the team with an impressive 40 goals and 29 assists. Mid-season, we suffered a season-ending injury to a starting defender and a change at the goalkeeper position. Josh Michaels, as backup goalkeeper, did a good job in a tough spot, leading the Indians to a 5–2 record.

Those two losses were tough ones: a defeat to Southern with nine seconds remaining, and a penalty-kick overtime loss to Northern in the West Region 1A Playoffs.

The change at goalkeeper came after a tough administrative decision to remove a goalkeeper from the team for having a rifle in a gun rack in his pickup truck parked on school grounds. It was an accident... a mistake to bring the rifle on campus. I thought the situation should have been treated differently because the rifle came on campus with no intent. Most trucks in Mount Savage had a gun rack with a rifle in it. The student-athlete was a nice young man. My hands were tied as the coach, and I totally understood. I just told the young man that life is not always fair, but that I am always here for him, and we will not forget the job he did as our starting goalkeeper this season.

Joe Shaffer was named Offensive Player of the Year for Western Maryland. Justin Weimer, O'Baker, and Moulden were selected to the All-Stars. Those six seniors did a great job and helped lead us to a 23–8 record over my first two years at Mount Savage.

The rumors about school consolidation continued, and they came to fruition the next school year. Little did we know, this would be the last year of Mount Savage High School soccer.

George was a great coach and an even better gentleman. George Bishields died in 2024, and I miss him.

Chapter 19: Consolidated

"I can't change the direction of the wind, but I can adjust my sails, always reaching my destination."

-Jimmy Dean

Team chemistry is the most underrated accomplishment of a team. We all thrive in a positive and collaborative environment.

Be careful when climbing the ladder and the impact it may have on your family. Consider all of the rungs.

Youth sports can suck.

Be aware of your players' fatigue at the end of the season.

Family is where our foundation lies. Build from that foundation.

Do not make rules just to have rules.

A small percent of teachers should not be working with children.

Don't be a helicopter parent, but be nearby in the bushes.

In the spring of 2000, the consolidation of Mount Savage High School and Beall High School was approved by the Allegany County Public Schools and began to take shape. The high school numbers at Mount Savage had dwindled. My best example was that only two freshman boy soccer players were on the junior varsity team during the

1998 fall campaign. Mount Savage and Beall had great academic and athletic traditions. It was decided that Mount Savage School would now house Mount Savage elementary and middle school students from both Mount Savage and Beall Schools. Beall High School would become the site for both Mount Savage and Beall High School students.

The official history of Beall High School, located in Frostburg, Maryland, is just five miles from Mount Savage, Maryland. Quite an easy commute for both locations and their students. In 1935, crowded conditions in Beall created the need for a new and larger high school building. The purchase of land from the Consolidation Coal Company on Eckhart Flat made it possible to build a new and more modern school. In 1935, "Beall High" was moved to a new location, which opened in January 1941. In 1984, the high school was completely renovated and remodeled.

As in all consolidated school situations, not all community members were in favor of the move. It is very difficult to lose any school, particularly a high school with its many activities and events that bring great quality and pride to any community. The same goes for faculty members at consolidated schools. The administration of Beall High School and the Allegany County Public Schools Board of Education would approve the move of any instructor or coach at the two schools. I was asked to move as a physical education teacher and boys' soccer coach from Mount Savage to Beall. I was excited about it, but also knew it would bring some drawbacks for me and my family. Whenever you make a move as a teacher or coach, you always have to consider the impact on your family.

Mount Savage and Beall High School had great notoriety as soccer schools over the years. As we opened our first August soccer practice for the fall season, it drew around 68 players. Amazing, right? We only had 24 uniforms for both junior varsity and varsity players. I would be required to cut over 20 players. I had hired coaches from both schools who knew most of the players prior to making some decisions that changed students' lives.

Never underestimate the impact on a student who made the team or was eliminated from it. I personally was cut from the junior varsity basketball team at Valley High School back in 1971. I always remember that night walking the railroad tracks home after my cut from the basketball team. I felt I had failed myself and my family. It was a sleepless night, but the sun came up the next day. I used that elimination from a team as a badge of courage in everything else I did in my life. As a coach of any team, always try to eliminate the cut system for young boys and girls. As my wife always says, "Youth sports suck."

Before we made our final cut, a new student arrived during a practice. He was from Ireland. His dad had come to Frostburg as an exchange instructor for Frostburg State University. The student's' dad introduced himself and his son. He said his son would like to try out for the team. I explained the situation with consolidation, but I would not deny him the chance. I asked him to take a corner kick as we were working on specialties at the time.

His name was Neil O'Driscoll. I asked Neil to place the corner kick between the 6 and 12 yard markers, known as the goal area and penalty mark. Neil asked me, "Who'se head do you want the ball placed on?"

I said, "Oh, okay, how about number 8's head?"

Neil delivered it right on 8's head.

"Can you do that again, but this time put it on number 6's chest?"

His dad said we have to leave for an appointment, but Neil could take one more kick. He put the ball right on number 6's chest. His dad said they needed to leave, and I told him we would see him tomorrow. Now I had another problem. Another student/athlete to add to the team.

We made our final cut that included disappointing 20 players from the team. Some players saw the writing on the wall and did not return after day one. The task created many coach meetings and many sleepless nights for me, remembering my own long walk up the railroad track when I was their age. To the credit of both parents of the two schools, I never had one complaint from an athlete or a parent. I told the student athletes who were cut that I had a similar experience when I was their age. The best thing to do is to use this decision as a motivator and devote all of your energy to your next challenge. Most importantly, make sure it is a positive challenge you can be proud of for you and your family.

14-0 Regular season

Even after the cuts, we had an opportunity to create a starting line-up for the varsity with 16 of the players from two schools and one player from Ireland who had been starters last year at their respective schools. This was a great problem to have. It gives you a sigh of relief after the pressure of tryouts and long hours as a coaching staff.

We knew we had talent, but could we have the athletes buy into supporting each other, believing in the process, and creating team chemistry? This situation would take a lot of instruction about pride, support, and loyalty. It would have to develop now and quickly. I spent every practice during and after each preseason meeting discussing each of these areas. I told the team to be positive toward each other. If you have to instruct another player on what they should have done in a particular situation, be firm but positive. We all make mistakes. But the mistakes we cannot tolerate are the ones we repeat. Learn from the mistake and grow.

The season began with a 9-0 win over Salisbury School in Pennsylvania. We actually recorded 6 straight shutouts to begin the season before we won 4-2 over Southern Garrett in Maryland. Neil O'Driscoll from Ireland was scoring goals like crazy. Back in Ireland, Neil was a defender and had only scored one goal in his young career. We went 14-0, recording an undefeated and untied season. Neil recorded 26 goals and 16 assists, and Cass Martin, who came from Mount Savage, had 22 goals on the season. Neil's 26 goals were a school record at Beall. We outscored the opponent 110 goals to 8 goals against.

The twelfth game of the season was against the school whose program I started, Bishop Walsh School. They were undefeated and came to our house. We beat the Spartans that night 3-1 in front of a packed house of 2400 fans. Many say that was the most fans at a soccer game in the tri-state area to date. That was a fun night for all of the Mountie fans.

It was a great season as the lads worked hard to build chemistry and support each other during the undefeated season. However, when the playoffs rolled around, we had one full week off because of our record and the points we had accumulated in Maryland Class 1A boys soccer. I thought we should keep the team together and work out, and only take Sunday off for practice. This was a big mistake on my part. When our first Region game rolled around, we lost to a team 1-2 that we had beaten in the regular season 7-3. It was obvious during the game that we had dead legs and had met our match that night in November. We had 16 corner kicks and could not muster up a good shot on goal.

At this point, I had a 175-116-10 record coaching soccer. I was given the Pepsi-Cola Award as Boys' Soccer Coach of the Year. We won the 1A West Region regular season title as well as the Western Maryland Interscholastic League (WMIL) title with a 5-0 record. Neil O'Driscoll was named player of the year, and Justin Weimer was named defensive player of the year. I would have to name the entire team as standouts for the team, other than these two players. They were all outstanding, and I will never forget that ""2000" season.

Over-preparation is a real thing in sports, and I was to blame. I felt bad for the boys, but was proud of their accomplishments of blending two school teams together to work as one. If ever there was a chance to win a state championship, I had just blown it.

Family is Important

I just read Tim Howard's book *The Keeper – A Life of Saving Goals and Achieving Them*. A great read for any soccer enthusiast. As a proven great goalkeeper for the United States National Soccer team, Manchester United, and Everton, he had gone so far in his life after being diagnosed with OCD (obsessive compulsive disorder) and TS (Tourette's Syndrome) at the young age of ten. He devoted his life to becoming one of the best goalkeepers in American soccer history. Tim had a great wife and two young children. He gave up his relationship with his wife, the mother of his children, because he was addicted to the game of soccer. He put a game before his family.

I love the game of soccer, and I have had a lot of successes and failures between the posts. But I have a wonderful wife and three beautiful boys who have lit up my life. Nothing could come between me and my family. I now have my wife, three sons, three wonderful daughters-in-law, and four grandchildren. Life could never be better. Did Tim Howard get it wrong?

During the fall of 2000, in the middle of that great Beall soccer season, I was approached by the principal to take on the girls' basketball team for the winter. I was hesitant because of what coaching takes away from your family. I discussed the idea with Lori and decided I should do it since I was coaching and teaching in the same school. These coaching stints are part-time contracts, but I wanted to be a team player for the Allegany County Public Schools.

As soon as the soccer season ended, I started coaching the girls' basketball team at Beall. They were a struggling program, coached recently by the same soccer coach who was moved to Mount Savage school to teach PE. The girls' team struggled, and we lost our first ten games before we registered a win. This humbled me after coaching an undefeated soccer season the fall prior. The girls worked hard and improved. We finished the season 6-16.

That spring, I applied for a Head Women's Soccer job at Erskine College in Due West, South Carolina. They flew me and my family to the Greensboro airport. The boys had their first airplane ride on this trip at ages ten, eight, and five.

Erskine College had set up an extensive interview process for the Saturday after our flight. Lori entertained the kids on campus while I had all-day interviews. That evening, the athletic director took our family out for dinner. On Sunday, we were escorted to the Presbyterian Church on campus since Eriskine is a Presbyterian College. This was a wonderful weekend for our family.

When we arrived back in Frostburg, Lori and I sat down and talked to the boys about our family making a move to Due West. We all decided that this was not the time and Due West was not the place to make a move. We had recently bought a new house in Frostburg, and the boys were feeling settled in their schools. I was still working on my Supervision and Administration Master's degree at Frostburg University.

Lori, the kids, and I had a great summer settling into our new house on James Court in Frostburg. I continued working with the soccer team outdoors during the summer. In Maryland Public School athletics, they allow you to train during the summer as long as a ball is not present. What a crock! If someone wants to spend time with our youth and keep them busy during the off-season, more power to them. Most of the time, the bureaucrats making the rules do not know a thing about educating and training our youth. They love to' make rules just to make rules.

Happy Homecoming?

I began my second year at Beall with the same excitement we had in the first. Well, minus Neil O'Driscoll from Ireland, who graduated last school year. Tough to replace a player who scored 26 goals and 16 assists. We still had the same enthusiasm, with a lot of participation, with some 50 players coming out for soccer in 2001. I told myself that I was going to try to have 2 junior varsity teams if the state would allow it. I did not want to keep cutting players each year. If you are on one of two junior varsity teams and you are not playing much, then you can decide if you want to continue with soccer or move on to another challenge.

We had a similar schedule and the same driven type of player at Beall in 2001. The only difference is that a lot of outside problems occurred that were beyond our control. They say only worry about the problems that you can control, but the issues we dealt with were concerning.

We got off to another great start with 9 wins in a row. One of our starting players and main linemen became sick. He was diagnosed with pulmonary hypertension. He was hospitalized and would spend the next two months there. This young man was a team favorite, and there wasn't a practice that 'went by that he was not in our prayers.

We finished the regular season with a 10-2-1 record. We won our first playoff game and were heading into a region semi-final game against state soccer power Williamsport High School. This was homecoming week for our football team. One of our Beall staff members found an alcohol citation on the floor in a school hallway. This citation was given to a football player. The staff member took it to the principal! This was a problem for the cited young man.

After an investigation by the school administration, it was found that a homecoming party had taken place and many fall sports athletes had attended. Evidently, our starting goalkeeper was one of those athletes attending the party. Our principal asked him if he was drinking alcohol at this party. The principal said if you say you did not and you play in tonight's game and I find out you did drink, we would forfeit the game should we beat Williamsport tonight. The young man admitted to making a poor decision and was suspended for the semi-final game.

As a coach, these things are beyond your control, but it's next man up. Travis Jackson was the next man up. Travis was loved by his teammates and coaching staff. We knew he would do a great job, and I had all the confidence in the world in Travis. I just wish we had had more of a notice, at least a day of practice, before throwing Travis into the hotbed.

When my wife arrived at the game, she knew something was wrong. Wife's intuition. She saw me pacing and rubbing my hands nervously from across the field.

It was a great soccer game, from one end to the other. Williamsport took a corner kick and beat one of our defensive players and headed the ball into the upper "90." Nothing Travis could have done differently on that ball. Keep all your defenders marked up on the release of the kick. After the kick, everyone has their own responsibility.

Travis Jackson did an outstanding job in the goal that night with some 10 saves. But a 1-0 score was enough to move Williamsport past Beall. I was proud of our team and especially Travis Jackson for his outstanding play that night.

We ended the 2001 campaign with a record of 11-3-1. Our player, who was hospitalized for months, was recovering and was able to attend our soccer banquet. His mother wheeled him into the banquet, and there was not a dry eye in the house. In my eyes, we had a second successful season at Beall, but the recovery of our teammate was the blessing of the 2001 season. That young man is healthy today and is very successful.

Off to the hardwoods to train our girls' basketball team at Beall. We had high expectations, and we had gained some confidence towards the end of last season. The girls were gelling, and we ended the season 9-11. The tide was turning, and the girls worked harder than ever. Sometimes, that 500 season eludes by one play, one call, or in this case, one game. I was exhausted following the back-to-back seasons.

Five Percent of Teachers Should Not Be Given The Responsibility of Working with Children!

My family was playing into my frustration and exhaustion with all the practices and games over the past 7 months. My oldest son Ross was falling victim to Mount Savage faculty and staff who were friends of the teacher/coach that I had replaced at Beall.

Lori and I received a letter from Mount Savage School stating that they were moving Ross from the top section in 7th grade. He had A and B grades since he had been at MSS. We spoke to Ross, and he did not understand the situation either. We were bewildered by this move and asked for a meeting. It appears an academic team of supporters of 'you know who' were making this decision. At our meeting, they told us that Ross was doing well with grades, but appeared nervous about school, and this move down a section would relax him. Lori and I read right through this team and said we wanted him to stay in the top section. We went to meet with the principal about the situation, and he knew nothing about Ross's movement. Ross remained in the top section and today has his Master's degree in business and is a program manager for Northrup Gruman.

The saga with Ross continued at Mount Savage School. A social studies teacher had given the class an assignment to create a video to present to the class. When it came Ross's turn to show the class his video, the teacher said, "Ross, you are next."

Ross said to the teacher, "You have my video, you said you would hold it for me."

The teacher said, "I do not have it. Go check your locker."

Ross came back without a video. The next day, the video appeared in Ross's locker. How did that happen? I told Ross that maybe he missed it the first time. He said, "I could not have."

A week later, this teacher was bragging at a county-wide social studies meeting about having Ross's video, but denying it. He said, "I got even with Ray Kiddy's son. I hid his son's video and then got into his locker and put it back in."

The teacher was laughing about it at the meeting. A fellow teacher at Beall was at the meeting and was disgusted by the game the teacher at Mount Savage played on my son. My friend said, "I don't care what you do with the information; you can even use my name."

I let the Mount Savage administration know what had happened, but I did not want anything done to the teacher. I could have pushed this to having that teacher suspended, moved, or fired.

Since Ross was only in 7th grade and had another year at the school, I dropped the situation. I never told Ross about what his teacher had done to him. I wanted him to grow up trusting and respecting his teachers. I finally told Ross after he graduated from high school.

Ross told me "he thought something strange had happened". Education has 5% of people in their workforce who should not be given the responsibility of teaching. Don't be a helicopter parent, but find some way to hover.

That winter, I applied at Shenandoah University to be the head women's soccer coach and women's and men's tennis coach. I was called by their administration for an interview and was awarded the job on a Friday. Shenandoah University was an hour and a half from Frostburg. I was excited about the position, and at this point, my current teaching/coaching position was causing my family problems. I talked to Lori and the boys about the position and making a move to Winchester, Virginia. Of course, no one was interested. So, Saturday and Sunday, I drove to Shenandoah University and back to Frostburg, Maryland, to see if I could commute from home. It was too far to do daily, and the conference that Shenandoah played in reached all the way down to the Carolina's and Florida.

I called the athletic directors at Shenandoah and apologized as I could not take this position. I was turning down a dream job where I would only have to recruit and coach young athletes. A full-time coaching position! The Shenandoah University administration tried to talk me into commuting from Frostburg and said I do not have to be on campus each day. You control your schedule. They were very generous with the offer, but I know that when I do a job, I throw myself into it 100%.

I completed my Master's' degree in Supervision in Administration that spring. I also applied to be an administrator in Allegany County Public Schools. I was offered an assistant principal position at Allegany High School. Greg Smith, my principal at Beall, came into my office after he heard I was offered a position.

He said, "Are you sure you are finished with coaching, because I do want to lose you."

I said, "Yes. After our homecoming debacle this fall, I want to be the guy in your position giving out the discipline, not the guy receiving the discipline of losing a goalkeeper two hours before a playoff game."

He said, "I totally understand."

For the fall of 2002, I became the Assistant Principal at Allegany High School!

Chapter 20: Rules and Regulations

"My friends are a bad influence, and I would like to thank them for that."

-Snoopy

Your children will learn from all of their coaches. The lesson learned may be how not to coach.

A school administration position is 24/7.

Chemistry among a team of school administrators can be fun. It had better be fun.

Before I was hired as Assistant Principal at Allegany High School, my superintendent and the HR supervisor asked me if I was finished with coaching. They needed to know, because an administrator's job is a 24/7 job. I said yes, but I was not sure it was completely out of my system.

I went on vacation that summer after my Assistant Principal interview. We went to the Outer Banks with the kids and had a great time. After a week of fun in the sun, I was checking the answering machine in June of 2002, following our vacation. One of those things you do to catch up back in the day when you have been out of circulation with phones, mail, family, friends, and colleagues. The HR director of

ACPS was on the voicemail asking me to give him a call. I called immediately, and the secretary said, "Yes, Ray, please hold."

The HR supervisor got on the phone and said, "Yes, Ray, how can I help you?"

"I am returning your call."

"Oh, I thought I talked to you yesterday."

"No, I have been away on vacation."

"I am sorry. Well, tonight the board of education will announce you as the Assistant Principal at Allegany High School. Sorry, I thought I already told you!"

"No problem, but I'm glad I found out before the announcement"!"

"He said, "No problem. Good luck!"

I was going to be the Assistant Principal at Allegany High School. That was the same school my dad would let me off at the door to watch the Alhambra Catholic Invitational Tournament. This was a basketball tournament that touted some of the best high school basketball in the country. Just to drop one name, Adrian Dantley says it all. I was twelve years old when Dad would drop me off for the tournaments three days in a row. Dad would pick me up after his mill working shift of 8 hours around 10:30pm. The gymnasium would be empty, and I would be a youngster with my program full of autographs, sitting in the dark on the front steps outside of Allegany by myself. Now I am going to be an administrator at this same school.

Of course, I was very familiar with Allegany High School, having coached three different sports at the school during my tenure in the same school system. I was going to work for Principal Mike Calhoun, whom I had tremendous respect for. Mike had been my Athletic Director and Assistant Principal during my prior years at Fort Hill and Beall, respectively. This would be Mike's first principalship. However, we were in good hands. Heidi Laupert was the other Assistant Principal at Allegany. She had taught English at Allegany and had been Assistant Principal for the past six years, giving us a heads-up on the makeup of the faculty and how they had operated in the past.

I set up my office with books on the shelf and keepsake paraphernalia in the window. I was set! I went to Mike and asked, "What do I do next?"

Mike said, "Be damned if I know, let's go see Heidi."

Boy, did we get an earful from Heidi on what to do next and what not to do. Heidi knew Allegany High School inside and out, so we just followed her lead.

Mike, Heidi, and I would form a good team for the next thirteen years as the administration of Allegany High School. We worked hard at supporting the students, faculty, and staff. We attended all extracurricular activities together. Oh yeah, and boy did we have fun together. This was a part of my life I will always cherish. Mike continued as principal at

Allegany until 2019, and Heidi became the Principal of Allegany until she retired in December of 20024. I retired from the ACPS and Allegany as Assistant Principal and supervisor of physical education and athletics in 2015.

Chapter 21: Caught the Bug Again

"The purpose of coaching is to close the gap between potential and performance."

-Keith Webb

The purpose of coaching takes on many turns during a career. I always found my purpose as a program builder. Sometimes the build was from scratch, and sometimes it was an entire renovation.

Keep your children busy, or they will find other things to do-look out!

A team has to be patient during the season as they mature and grow as a group.

There is nothing more satisfying than stealing a victory when the opponent was more talented than you.

Regrets build you for the next challenge.

Working as an Assistant Principal at Allegany High School was challenging, and I was enjoying the type of responsibility. Ross, my oldest son, decided to attend Allegany as a freshman in 2004. He played American football and tennis. Since 2002, I had been a volunteer coach supporting my sons in youth soccer, youth football, and even served as President of the Frostburg Cougar Football Club for two years. We played travel soccer, indoor soccer, and basketball camps throughout the school years. I enjoyed working with my sons and their friends in sports. Oh yeah, by the way, I also began a Doctorate program in 2001 and earned my Doctor of Sports Psychology in Applied Sports Psychology through The Optimal Performance Institute and University in Sunnyvale, California, in May of 2005

Keep your children busy. If you do not keep them busy, they will find other things to do-look out!

I was at a basketball camp with my sons when Bob Kirk, the athletic director and outstanding JUCO basketball coach at Allegany College, stopped me in the hallway of the local YMCA and asked me if I would want to coach the Allegany College of Maryland men's soccer team. I was honored to be offered such a position since Coach Kirk was like a father to me when I was a student athlete at Allegany Community College. He was also an outstanding AD and B-Ball coach, being named in the National Junior College Hall of Fame in Grand Junction, Colorado. ACC became Allegany College of Maryland in the fall of 1996. I told Coach Kirk that I was honored and would think about it.

Allegany College of Maryland, formerly ACC, had two other coaches in the National JUCO Hall of Fame. They were Steve Bazarnic, baseball coach, and Dr. Glenn Workman in the sport of Tennis. Quite a feat for a small JUCO school with an enrollment of 1800 students. Today, ACM has 2500 students.

That Monday, I went to my principal, Mike, to see what his thoughts were on me coaching at the local college. First response was "Why not!"

He was always supportive of me and the suggestions I had made as Assistant Principal. He said, "Let me run it by the superintendent just so there are no surprises." Mike got back to me that afternoon and said, "Go for it, we have the superintendent's blessing."

I knew this would mean a lot of additional hours for me, already covering two or three nighttime activities a week in my assistant principal position.

I was named the ACM men's soccer coach in the winter of 2006. Allegany had not been able to field teams the past two years due to a lack of eligible players. We were starting from scratch. However, Darrell Blank, my college coach, who had led the Trojans since 1975, accepted the offer to be my assistant coach for the 2006 season. Coach Blank guided ACM to Maryland JUCO Division A titles in 1982 and 1988. He was Region XX Coach of the Year in 1982 and Maryland Coach of the Year in 1996. Allegany had its best season with a 12-5 record in 1994 and set school records for most wins (12) and most goals scored (59). I loved Coach Blank and respected him as a coach and teacher when I was a student at ACM. I was excited to work with him again.

In early 2006, we started the spring season. It consisted of three practices a week, and we traveled to tournaments. One was held by a Maryland JUCO team, and one was against four-year schools at Westminster College in New Wilmington, PA, where I coached soccer for six weeks. It was good to visit that campus again. The surprise of the spring season was that Sebastian Lyons, a goalkeeper from Prince

George's County in Maryland, was planning to attend ACM. He and his dad drove two and a half hours to Cumberland two days a week to work out with us. We didn't recruit Sebastian; he recruited us. He was a great goalkeeper and an outstanding young man to work with. He stood 6'1 and weighed some 230 pounds. However, he could float like a butterfly and sting like a bee. I don't know who said that first!

The fall season practices opened the last week of August 2006. We had a good group of local talent and some players like Sebastian from out of the area. One highlight was Manny Mensah from Ghana, who was an outstanding center back. Those two were joined by locals Chris Herath, Donnie Ellsworth, and Brian Jefferies from Cumberland, Tommy Norris from Frostburg, Joe Brady, and Tyler Bollman from Bedford, Pennsylvania. Also, Rene Lafuente of Springfield, Virginia. The twenty-one players created excitement for our squad because we had a great work ethic at practice. Our only downfall would be their inexperience at the college level because we had not had a team for the past two seasons.

We are Competitive

We faced a difficult schedule with a number of teams from the Maryland JUCO Conference that were nationally ranked. I was hopeful we would show steady progress throughout the season and surprise some teams.

We started out with a good 2-1 win over Hagerstown Junior College. The next game was against nationally ranked Prince George's

Community College, which held an early-season national ranking. The game was at their place. This was also a chance for Sebastian Lyons, our goalkeeper, to go home. We were outmanned and they overpowered us in the second half, beating us 8-0. Ouch!

As we headed to the locker room with our tails between our legs, Sebastian asked Coach Blank, "How many saves did I have, Coach Blank?"

Coach Blank said, "Five."

Well, despite the score, Sebastian played a great game. He and Manny were on defense the entire second half, and we were lucky we only gave up 6 goals that half. Sebastian was a nice young man, but he went off on Coach Blank, even using profanity. Uncharacteristic of Sebastian. I tried to settle him down. Coach Blank started to explain the definition of a save, and Sebastian said I know what the "f*** a save is, I have been between the pipes for the past 12 years, you idiot."

I finally calmed Sebastian down, and we showered. We were on the bus. I had to laugh about the scorebook follies. I thought of the exchange between a player and a coach. I liked the fight that Sebastian had in him. I also knew I had to talk to the team at the next practice about patients during the season and how we would mature and grow as a group. I needed them as a team to support each other when the chips were down and to believe in our process.

In Sebastian's defense, he probably had five saves in the first five minutes of that ninety-minute game.

Sebastian and Darrell Blank never kissed and made up, but they tolerated each other the remainder of the season. We won our next two games and then had to play number 3 in the country, Montgomery Community College. They were a huge school. Back in those days, they had enrollment numbers that equaled the University of Maryland. We practiced parking the bus, stuffing shots from 18-24 yard shooting range, and having patience on fouls around midfield to give us opportunities on offense.

When you park the bus in soccer, you rely on the counterattack when possible. You have to have a fast, direct attack that occurs when a team transitions from defense to offense. You are aiming to capitalize on the opponents' vulnerability before they can regroup.

At the end of the first half, the score was 0-0, and I could see Montgomery was frustrated. I pointed out that we cannot give up an early goal in the first half. Eight minutes into the second half, they scored to go up 1-0. Way too early! However, we settled in and stuck with our game plan. With six minutes to go into the game, we got a clear and a breakaway. The ball floated in the air to Brian Jefferies, who headed the ball to Donnie Ellsworth, who headed the ball into the upper ninety of Montgomery's net. Nothing like a double header in the game of soccer on offense. This caught their defense off guard and on their heels, and we had knotted the game 1-1.

Sebastian and Manny headed off their offense for the remainder of the game and two overtime periods. We played outstanding as a team, followed the game plan, and pulled a 1-1 tie with the nationally ranked Dragons. As I watched our guys celebrate and run off the field, it was one of my proudest moments as an underdog team that had just stolen a win away from a nationally ranked team. We were now 3-1-1, and the team is growing with confidence. My thought was that this should be fun for the remainder of the season.

Brian Jeffries was another highlight for the season. He tied the school scoring record. Brian scored 13 goals and tied a school record set by Jeff Harbel, who scored 13 goals in 1999 for the Trojans.

We struggled after a great start and were 6-4-3 with three games remaining. Coach Blank came to our next practice and told me we needed to win one game out of the last three remaining games to be entered in the Region XX playoffs. I felt this was a reasonable decision. Each school in Region XX can enter the playoffs by paying three hundred dollars. Despite your record, pay the fee, and you are in. I felt the decision by our AD was fair. I told the players about our task, but also told them this was a tall request. We had Harford, Anne Arundel, and Howard remaining, respectively. They were all good teams.

We lost to Harford and had Anne Arundel next! I went to practice before the Anne Arundel game, and Coach Blank said that one of our players the night before this game had parked in a staff-only space. He said our AD was upset about this and was going to suspend the player for tomorrow's game with AA. I thought, 'You have got to be kidding me!' We practice at 4:00pm, and those six spaces are all empty. Should a player park there? No. But without a warning, it is not worth the penalty of suspension. I respect all administrations and let the player know that he could not play tomorrow. He was a starter and a difficult loss to our team, with having to win one game out of two to enter the playoffs. We lost the AA the next day.

One game to go against Howard Community College, and everything was on the line. Coach Blank came to the practice before the Howard game and said he and our Athletic Director had decided we would not enter the Region XX playoffs, whatever the outcome of tomorrow's game.

I said, "What? You cannot change the rules in the middle of the game, and our kids are fired up to win the game tomorrow."

Darrell said, "That is a final decision." I asked Darrell to get practice started. He asked, "Why"?"

I said, "I am going in to see the AD!"

Darrell said, "Oh, Ray, don't, he will not want to talk to you!" Like he was the wizard of Oz behind the curtain.

I marched into the AD's office and asked the secretary if I could talk to Bob Kirk. She said, "He is very busy, but let me see if I can get you in." She did, and he said to send Ray in. I asked about the new decision about my soccer team and not going into the playoffs, despite tomorrow's outcome. Bob said, "That is a final decision, and we would have to feel you could win it all in order to put you into the playoffs."

I asked if I had any input into this decision. He said, "The decision is final. We do not award mediocrity at ACM."

Ouch, that hurt! I shook his hand and said it was nice working with you.

I returned to practice and took over where Darrell was in the practice schedule. I was hot, fuming, and trying to think how I was going to break this news to the players. After about twenty minutes, Bob Kirk came out to our practice and motioned with his hand for me to come see him. I went over to Bob, hoping he had changed his mind.

Bob said, "Ray, don't get me wrong, you have done a good job this season."

I said, "No, you said I did a mediocre job. I will coach tomorrow and the next season to see my players I recruited through their graduation and to complete their eligibility."

He asked if that is how I want this to end.

I said, "That is my final decision."

Over a Measly Three Hundred Dollars

I never told the players about a new decision about playoffs during or after practice. I did not want the players to give up on our team. They were fired up, and I knew we would beat Howard tomorrow.

As we warmed up the next day, our AD was on a golf cart up by the gym, ready to watch the game. Our team fought hard, and with ten minutes remaining in the game, we scored to take a 1-0 lead. I looked for our AD while our guys celebrated, and Bob Kirk had driven his golf cart away. We held on to win the game 1-0, and I had to walk over and gather my players who were celebrating their hard-fought victory.

I congratulated the players and broke the news about not going into the playoffs. I started to cry as I made the statement that you have been screwed by this administration, and it is not fair, but as we all know, life is not fair sometimes. The players were disappointed and said, "This is not over, coach."

I wished it was not, but I knew it was over. The players tried to group parents together to put pressure on the administration. The man behind the curtain was final with his decision.

We ended the season 7-6-3 and never entered the Region XX playoffs. We held up our end as a team, and I was proud of our team for that.

I attended the Region XX meeting for playoff seeding and selection of All Stars. The other coaches could not believe we did not enter the playoffs. The coaches voted me Region XX Coach Of The Year. I was humbled to be honored by coaching peers. I would trade that award to have the team enter the playoffs if I could. Our team worked so hard to turn the program around. Prior to the Region XX Championship game, I coached the Maryland JUCO Men's JUCO Conference Division III sophomores in the soccer All-Star at the University of Maryland, Baltimore County (UMBC).

Through the spring, I recruited only local players because only I knew that year two at ACM would be my last. I wanted to put everything into the next season, but I did not feel it was right to recruit a player to come a long way from home. That athlete would only have one season with me as the coach. No one and done for me.

That spring, I entered our ACM team into the YMCA indoor soccer league. I also started conducting clinics for their youth and soccer coaches. This was very rewarding to give back to my community. These clinics were open to the public and were always free. Probably one of the most rewarding soccer things I have ever done.

Tough Times

We started the season for year two at ACM with high hopes. I knew we were not as talented as the year prior because we lost some fine young men to graduation. Manny Mensah was enrolled in a health program that took him away from practices two nights a week and several games due to a late afternoon lab. Sebastian Lyons was returning, but I think those returning had a bad taste in their mouth from the season prior. I tried to be as upbeat as I could.

The bottom line was we struggled and finished the season 5-10-1. We lost four games in overtime. I never mentioned the playoffs the entire season. I approached each game by staying focused and improving as a team. The season came and went, and I departed ACM. My only regret for my alma mater is that I wish I had had a longer career. I received more from ACM during my playing days than I gave them as a coach. Sometimes, regrets build you up for the next challenge.

Acute Stroke!

In December of 2007, two days before the Christmas break, I suffered a stroke in my office at Allegany. I was the only administrator in the building, and it was a busy school day. I found drugs in a student locker and informed the police to report to the school. I also had a probation officer in my office when I felt very dizzy. Dave Winter, the probation officer, called for the health nurse. The next thing I knew, I was hospitalized. Two of my sons, Ross and Garrett, were students at Allegany that day. You can imagine the fear they had when they heard the news that I was being transported in an ambulance.

After four days of hospitalization, the team of doctors notified me that I had suffered an acute stroke and had lost one of my brain stems. People usually have four; I now have three. This was eighteen years ago, and I am very fortunate. I have some loss of balance, but other than that, I am fully recovered. I am blessed!

Chapter 22: Worst Assistant Coach Ever

"The easiest thing to do is to criticize others. Might as well compare yourself."

-Ray Kiddy

The easiest thing to do in life is to criticize others. We will get nowhere if all we do is criticize.

There is so much to learn as an assistant from the head coach.

Be a good role model. Your players want to look up to you. Don't get a red card!

If you fail, pick yourself up and come up swinging smarter.

Since I became the Assistant Principal at Allegany High School, I had the coaching twitch, but I only itched it when coaching my sons during indoor and spring soccer seasons. Then I scratched that itch by taking on Allegany College of Maryland for two years. You know how that turned out. But in 2008, my middle son was entering his junior year of high school. Our soccer coach at Allegany, Rick Zimmerman, asked me to be his assistant for the Campers that year. I wasn't sure what the Allegany County Board of Education would say, but I was ready to check it out! I asked my boss, Mike Calhoun, the Principal of Allegany, to get his opinion. Mike loved the idea and got the approval from the superintendent.

It didn't hurt that one BOE member had a son on the Allegany team. I was excited because I had been coaching other teams during the fall season when my sons were playing. I missed working with them during those fall seasons; however, this year I could work with Garrett's team. Just being at every practice and game was going to be great for me and my family, or so I thought!

I always built teams through the culture first. When you are the assistant coach, it is someone else's culture. You can help the head man shape that culture, but it is the head man's culture. Garrett worked hard as usual, but I was always cautious that it might be too much pressure provided by me. I asked to work with the keepers to give Garrett and his teammates space from me during that time. I think that worked, but that was in my view only.

This would be only my third time as an Assistant Soccer Coach in my 25 years thus far. I hope I was a good assistant for Vince at IUP in 1985 (6-8-3) and Jay Hageman at Frostburg State University back in 1990. We finished 14-5-1, and I feel I had good input for the Bobcats. What I really know is that I learned a lot from Vince, Jay, and Rick. Vince worked his team hard and was great at judging his personnel. Jay was smart, patient, and moved his teams in a positive way. He was quick to listen, slow to speak, and also slow to become angry as a coach in the heat of battles. I respected his traits and tried to follow his lead.

First Red Card Ever

I started my third assistant coaching stint with thoughts of Vince and Jay's lessons in my preparation. Rick Zimmerman and I played on the same teams at Allegany College of Maryland. Rick loved soccer when he played, and I knew he would bring the same enthusiasm when he coached. He was well organized and had his players' best interests in mind. As his assistant, I had the same goals as Rick, but I thought I saw through some individual players' own agendas that he did not see. As the coach, in any team sport, you have to be aware of players who are not team players. Those individual agendas will bring down the team chemistry and can spread like wildfire during a twelve-week season.

During a regular-season game late in the season, I received a red card. There was an obvious handball in the penalty box in front of our bench. I was irate. The official walked toward me, and I said to him, "You cannot move that ball out of the penalty area, and I guess you are going to give me a yellow card."

He continued to walk toward me and said, "No, I am going to give you a red card."

He did, and I was the first person ever to be ejected from a new high school stadium at Mountain Ridge High School. Not a proud moment! The announcer, who was an assistant coach of mine at one time, announced that the Doctor had left the building. I was embarrassed for my son, my family, and my team. This was my first red card as a player or coach and would be one of only two red cards in my playing/coaching career. I was wrong and paid the price by sitting out the next game. I watched that game from my car in the parking lot as a parent rooting for Garrett. We all make mistakes, and this was a mistake on my part. I am sorry, Garrett!

Be a good role model. Your players want to look up to you. Don't get a red card!

Our players played hard that season. We lost to a good team in region play when a late corner kick went off one of our defenders' backs and into the goal. It was in a crowded goal box, which was unfortunate for this player. We lost that game 2-1 on that goal. That player did not come back to Allegany the following Monday for school after that unfortunate goal. In fact, he never returned to Allegany High School again. I tried calling parents, grandparents, and the athlete himself. But I failed! Not sure what the student athlete's mindset was in this situation. The only thing I know is that this was a good player who had an unfortunate ball bounce the wrong way. When that happens to you, you bounce back and hope the next ball will go your way. We missed that player the following season.

We finished that season 9-5-1, and I felt Rick Zimmerman had done an overall excellent job as the head coach. I failed as an assistant coach in so many ways that year. I am the worst assistant coach ever! At the end of the season, I was determined to do a better job as assistant coach. If you fail, pick yourself up and come up swinging smarter.

Going To Camp At Age Fifty-two

In the summer of 2009, Coach Zimmerman worked with the boys during a summer league through the YMCA. I decided to up my game by attending the National Soccer Coaching Association Academy at Bloomsburg University in Pennsylvania. This was to earn my National Coaching Diploma. This academy ran from Monday, July 6, to Sunday, July 12, 2009. I was fifty-two years old, and this was quite a challenge for me physically. I was one of the three oldest coaches at the academy. There were only two older than me.

The NSCAA Academy was very well organized and put us through physical training and classroom work for about 9.5 hours per day. We were separated into coaching groups of eight. I had a good team of coaches, and we made it as much fun as we could during the stressful challenge. I made up a checklist of how to get good grades as a soccer player for one of my three presentations during the academy. The list included the following, with other details as a project:

- Believe in Yourself
- Be Organized
- Manage Your Time Well
- Take Good Notes
- Study Smart
- Have Test-Taking Strategies
- Reduce Test Anxiety

- Get Help When You Need It.

I felt good about going through the academy, especially at an older age. It gave me great insight into the current movement of soccer. Soccer was changing to more of a mental game, encouraging our athletes to think faster with decision-making.

I also took the School Leadership Series test that summer. This was a national test to score your ability in evaluation of actions, synthesis of information, problem solving, analysis of information and decision making. I passed the test, but was all worn out with schooling for the summer of 2009. I couldn't wait for August 15, 2009, to start the fall soccer season at Allegany High School.

We started the season on a good note, beating some top-level teams. Coach Zimmerman was putting the boys through the paces, and you could see improvement throughout the season. I was trying to be a better assistant, but I now know too much and was trying to guide Rick as much as I could.

We won the Appalachian Mountain Athletic Conference (AMAC) soccer championship with a final season win over Keyser High School. I was one of the administrators to form and finalize the new conference three years prior. Garrett and I were excited about winning the AMAC Championship.

Coach Zimmerman said, "If we beat KHS tomorrow night, I am treating everyone to McDonald's on the bus ride home."

We won, and Garrett and I rushed to the bus, and the only one on the bus was Coach Zimmerman. All the players went home with their parents. The bus ride home was me, Garrett, Coach Zimmerman, and the bus driver. We didn't stop at McDonald's, and Garrett and I went home and had Lori's victory pizza.

We finished the season 10-4-1 with a tough loss to Clear Spring in the playoffs, 2-1. I enjoyed those two years working with the ALCO team and, most importantly, working with my son, Garrett. Some of our better players during those two seasons were Ryan Alderson, Adam Boor, Jaron Lutton, Ryan Marchini, Collin Sainz, and Luke Thompkins. I tried to be a good assistant, but it is just not a good position for me. Sorry, Vince, Jay, and Rick!

Chapter 23: A Labor of Love

""Once a JUCO, always a JUCO""

-Ray Kiddy

I loved coaching junior college soccer. The junior college athletes love playing the game.

When you love your coaching job, the time you pour into it seems like minutes.

As a coach or parent, you are not their friend or buddy. Save the latter for later. They are craving discipline.

You never win an argument with an official when he or she has made their decision. Save your energy!

A coaching staff has to have team chemistry

Remember, when you hire someone, you may have to fire them someday.

A loss of life, there is no recovery.

A New Beginning!

Following my assistant soccer coaching stint at Allegany High School, I was searching for another challenge. Garrett was going to graduate next May, and we needed to search for a college for him as well. Our oldest son, Ross, was attending West Virginia University in the Sports Management program. I took Garrett and his friend and teammate to see a Potomac State College men's soccer game. They were playing Southern Maryland College from Charles County, Maryland.

Garrett wanted to continue playing college soccer, but also wanted to join Ross at WVU. The game we witnessed at Potomac State College was a trouncing 9-0 by Southern Maryland. Neither of the boys was impressed. However, while I was at the game, the PSC Athletic Director came up to me and started talking. I had known Shawn White just by being involved in athletics in the tri-state area. He asked me if I would be interested in coaching at Potomac State. He said the head coach was giving the job up at the end of the season and asked me if I would apply. I started salivating like a dog that was just offered a ham bone.

On the way home, I asked the boys what they thought about the game and Potomac State College. They both said they would not want to attend PSC. I knew it would not be an easy place to recruit; however, they had some success in soccer in 2005-2007 when Patrick Brett was their coach. Patrick Brett won 24 games in his last two years at PSC, and they were ranked as high as 12 nationally during those two years. They made it to the national tournament twice when I was coaching at Allegany College of Maryland. Not too shabby for a small college that only had men's soccer since the year 2000.

Potomac State College is a Junior College that is located in Keyser, West Virginia. PSC was created in 1901 as the "Keyser Preparatory Branch of the West Virginia University" to assist the area in secondary education. The college is a fully integrated division of West Virginia

University offering over sixty degree programs and nine athletic sports, including esports (co-ed). They offered football until 1999 and added men's and women's soccer in 2000.

Well, that salivating dog went home, refreshed his resume, and wrote a cover letter. You are probably wondering how many times this old dog scratched that soccer itch. I sent the information to the PSC AD the next morning. About a week later, I heard from Shawn White, and he wanted me to come in for an interview. I was excited, just like my wife when she smells fresh-cut lumber for a new home being built.

You know the story: I interview and get the job, and I am ready to jump on the recruiting trail. Many things to do when you start up a JUCO versus a high school continuation program. The list just keeps growing, but I must start with recruiting since I was already a fall season behind. I could still catch the playoffs and all-star games to wind down the end of the past regular season.

Shawn White also offered the men's soccer team a field house that was occupied by the baseball team on the east side of the building. As I toured the soccer side, I was amazed at how run-down the facility had become! However, it started my wheels turning and thinking about all of the possibilities. Can I renovate this field house, along with putting together a competitive team for the fall of 2010? Only with the help of my sons and a lot of sweat and tears.

The field house had been a warehouse for everything but soccer gear and had a golf driving and putting area. This area could be cleaned out since the golf team did not use the area that winter. However, the grass seed stored in this area for athletic fields was overrun by the local mice. They would eat the grass seed and drink water until their bellies would expand to the point that they would explode. Shawn told me he would pay for paint, cleaning supplies, and some small renovations. He did not mention critter extermination.

Renovations

My sons would help me after school with renovations. Ross was in college, but would dedicate his weekends to working on the field house. In fact, he spent his entire spring break working on the field house. We had to wear masks because of the dead carcasses of the mice. It was quite a sight. The cleanup was the worst, but then it was full steam ahead. I was recruiting and renovating in the evening. By day, I was still assistant principal at Allegany High School. I was working some 14-16 hours a day and loved every minute of it.

During the winter, I organized the team members from the fall (2009) and had them play indoor soccer two nights a week in the gym. I arranged for the team to travel to Davis and Elkins to play in a futsal tournament. The guys were excited about playing other competitors, instead of beating each other up during the winter practices. Ross helped me with driving and coaching that weekend. I was amazed at what he knew about soccer and how he could communicate with the lads. My thoughts were that he was learning a lot at WVU through the sports management program. I was proud of him that weekend because he really did not know the players, but he earned their respect with his encouragement and direction.

Following winter practices, we moved outdoors for spring ball two days a week. Our outdoor field was an old football field that needed a lot of work. However, I was getting smarter; my plate was full. If it weren't for my sons assisting in every way possible, we would be two months behind in every area.

The students were going home for the summer. I needed to meet with each returning player to tell them my expectations for them, and to also meet with the sophomores who were moving on to thank them for the winter/spring campaign and invite them to the fall season alumni game. This was a great group of student-athletes.

Summer was upon me. I continued recruiting, following up on summer workouts with recruits and returning players. I always had a workout for the athletes to follow each week. This included a Cooper Test—a twelve-minute run test that measures a person's aerobic fitness and cardiovascular endurance. It was designed by Kenneth H. Cooper in 1968 for the U.S. Military. The measured distance divides a four-hundred-meter track into eighths, and you record the number of laps and number of eighths you completed in 12 minutes. For example, 5 laps and 3/8's of a lap. I had the athletes record and send me their results every two weeks to see how they were progressing over the summer. If they followed my other weekly workouts, they would improve their fitness level. Sure, they could embellish their summer reporting, but I had a built-in lie detector. I tested the athletes the first week back.

I also had to find another assistant coach for the fall season. Ross was doing an internship with our team for his sports management program. This was great having Ross, but the budget allowed for another part-time assistant. I was able to reunite with Brad Burr, who assisted me at Fort Hill High School back in 1992 & 93. Remember, Brad had great teams at Fort Hill in 1994 and 95. They were area soccer champs in 1994, and Coach Burr was named Dapper Dan Pepsi Cola Coach of the Year. Brad was retired and looking for another challenge, and was excited about helping at Potomac State College. Brad is a great human being, loves kids, and was eager to help out with coaching. Most importantly, Brad was a great organizer and had a good ear for me to bounce off ideas of activities and personnel.

August arrived, and by the second week, the athletes were ready to go. The field house looked great, and players were excited to have their own space. I set up a desk for any player who had fallen behind in studies so they could focus on class work and not soccer. You were sidelined when you fell behind, and you did seat time studying at that desk. No games for you that week. I always stressed the importance of academics.

As a coach or parent, you are not their best friend or buddy. Save the latter for later. They are craving discipline.

Our two finest soccer recruits were Juan Flores from Stonewall Jackson High School, Virginia, and Riccardo Murphy from Maya

221

Angelou Public Charter High School, Washington, DC. These two players could flat-out play and were immediate starters for our team as freshmen. Our schedule included fifteen games with six four-year schools.

Smoking Guns

Our first game was against Gallaudet University. Gallaudet University is a private federally chartered university in Washington, DC. It is for the deaf and hard of hearing. Our charter bus was provided by West Virginia University and was plush. When I arrived to put equipment on the bus, my goalkeeper was smoking a cigarette outside the bus. You have got to be kidding me! He was a 6 foot five, 250-pound man who spent his first years out of high school in the Marines. A good goalkeeper!

I said, "What are you doing?"

He said he smoked to relax before a game. I said, "Put that cigarette out and do not let me see you smoke ever again."

On another road trip, the big old Marine wanted to do the wing challenge at Buffalo Wild Wings in Winchester, Virginia. The challenge is eating as many spicy hot wings as you can in ten minutes. These are the hottest of hot wings. Mike put them down, and you could see steam coming out of his nose, and—I thought—his ears. Okay, exaggeration. He then downed a quart of milk, and we went home. I love JUCO players. Of course, the Marine met the challenge.

Our best win that season was over Anne Arundel, 2-1. AA was coming off a good win against Southern Maryland, a JUCO Division 1 school. Ross had scouted them against Allegany College and followed their stats, so we felt good going into this game. We were a Division III JUCO school. That meant you did not dish out scholarships or room and board. Players were there because of love for the game.

We played in the Region XX JUCO tournament against Prince George's Community College in the first round. We lost that game 5-0, and we were never in the game. Our backup goalkeeper injured his shoulder, and we spent most of the evening at Prince George's Community Hospital. Our wing-eating ex-marine broke his leg in the last game of the season, hence the backup. Ross took the players to eat dinner while I stayed at the hospital. Ross said taking the team in the van was scary because he took a side street in Prince George's County; he thought it was a one-way road. We got home around 3 in the morning. The life of JUCO coaches.

Our team captains, John Schneider, Riley Harrold, and Eliud Vega, led us to a winning mark that first season, 8-6-1. Riley and Ricardo Hunter were both named to the Region XX second team. I was never prouder of a group, including Brad and my three sons, to pull off a field house renovation and a solid first year of soccer at Potomac State College. I think I will stay here a while!

Building The Second Year

The following season, Brad, Ross, and I began recruiting immediately. We did some recruiting during the past fall season, but it is difficult as part-time coaches—preparing practices, games, travel, meals, and overall parenting a team, who are away from home, eats away at all your time—let alone being an Assistant Principal at another school.

We knew we needed to increase our numbers since we were graduating ten sophomores. That is when I thought, why not throw on our plate, improving our grass field. Brad loved the idea and tracked down his friend Phil Mills. Phil was the golf turf expert at the Cumberland Country Club in Cumberland, Maryland. Phil came down and gave us some advice and a helping hand.

One day in November, following the fall season, we were to do a late fall season seed. When I arrived, Ross and Brad had already started. I had just come from my full-time job. Shawn White had arranged for maintenance to loan us a tractor that looked like it was on Henry Ford's assembly line with the quadricycle in 1896. Brad had a drag on the back of the tractor and stopped to see if I wanted a try on the old goat. I said, "Sure."

Brad told me how to start the critter and how to put it in gear. He said it was hard to get in gear. I put it in gear. Brad was standing between the tractor and the drag, and I knocked him ass over a tin cup. The drag went over Brad. I looked back, and Brad motioned to keep going, and Ross took Brad to the field house to attend to his injuries.

I kept moving, but was worried about Brad, and we were also working against daylight. Ross and my other two sons are all Boy Scouts of America Eagle Scouts. I knew Brad was in good hands. I kept dragging away, and after about an hour, Brad came out of the field house. Ross had Brad bandaged up, in a sling, and using a cane. Joint wounds were the most dangerous injuries during the Civil War. Brad looked like he had come off a battlefield. Fortunately, he did not lose any extremities. Other than a tongue lashing, this was the first time one of my assistants suffered bodily harm.

We recruited hard that winter and spring. The weight room activities were added by Ross twice a week, along with our indoor soccer practices. We continued through our routine spring practices. Incoming freshmen were allowed to work out one day with us during the spring practices. It was nice to see how things would come together as a unit.

May came quickly, and we felt good about our recruitment. I always felt good in numbers with recruitment if I had a list of 45 possible players by December and 75 by March. These numbers seem like a lot, but when you finalize your call to make sure who is coming, the list can dwindle quickly. Sometimes, ten in a row on the list have had other offers or have changed their mind about going to college at all.

The second week of August came quickly, and on that first day, we had 38 players report to camp. My list said forty, but you can lose about five percent, never arriving. I wanted to recruit effectively to make us better in the second year, but more importantly, to assist the college with enrollment.

Thirty-eight was too many players to carry on the team. First, I did not have that many uniforms. Brad and I decided to redshirt five players and cut five players. Twenty-eight was still a large number on our team, but I thought we could manage. We had upped the schedule to eighteen games, and that gave some wiggle room for additional playing time.

I couldn't recruit Garrett my first year at PSC, but my second year he did leave WVU and attended Potomac. He missed playing soccer. I was glad he came to PSC. That first day, Brad said he never saw Garrett so happy. Ross said that was because he was the only one out there who knew he had made the team.

Garrett was also working as an RA in his dorm and was proud of his leadership role. With Garrett's GPA from WVU and his community service through scouting, he was a shoo-in for the position. I did not have to bend anyone's elbow. He got the position on his own.

It Came Down to Blows

My second season started out with three wins before we lost our first game to a good College of Southern Maryland team. Our team was playing well and we had surpassed my expectations until we lost a mid-season game to Anne Arundel Community College 2-0. During that game, Riccardo Murphy, our top forward, was being marked tightly by AACC. With ten seconds remaining in the first half in front of our bench,

Riccardo was bumped from behind by a defender, and he turned around and punched the defender. Five players on the bench stepped on the field and grabbed Riccardo to restrain him. When the dust had settled, Riccardo and my bench players who had stepped onto the field were ejected from the game and had to go to their dormitories for the second half.

This was a blow to our team, and we never recovered in the second half, suffering the 2-0 loss. Most notable was that the ejected players could not play the next game. My argument with the official was that my players who left the bench were not aggressors, but just tried to subdue their teammate. You never win an argument with an official when they have made their decision. Coaching rule number one!

The highlight of the regular season was a tight loss to nationally ranked Montgomery Rockville. We took an early lead 1-0 on a Riccardo Murphy goal off an assist from Zachary Saylor. Montgomery scored two second-half goals, with the winning goal coming with 3 minutes remaining in the game. Conor Fungaroli, our keeper, had an outstanding game, recording 9 saves. It was a close, contested game. Of course, we wanted to win, but it was a good effort by our guys. It showed we could have an impact against teams nationally. They were a team we were going to have to go through to get to the nationals.

Our first round of the Region XX playoffs would pit us against Anne Arundel at their place. We badly wanted to win that game after having somewhat of a melee in that 0-2 loss during the regular season. This was a quarter-final playoff game. We were focused during the two practices before the AACC game. I felt the boys wanted it, and we could secure our first playoff win during my tenure. We turned the tables and beat AACC 2-0. The boys were pumped on the way home.

The next day, we learned we would play Montgomery Rockville in the Region XX semifinal. We had one day to prepare, and it was a so-so practice. I felt the boys looked tired, and after all, it was November. That JUCO soccer season is fast and furious, but it can take its toll on a team. The advantage we had was that we had 28 players on the roster. We played hard, only giving up one goal in the first half to Rockville. We thought if we could hold them scoreless in the second half, we could get lucky against their stubborn defense. We came up short, and the 2011 season ended with a 0-1 loss to the fifth-ranked team in the nation.

The 2011 season finished with a 10-5-1 record. We recorded our first Region XX playoff win. We outscored our opponent 46-20. Conor Fungaroli finished 10th in the country with 0.94 (less than one goal per game) goals against, allowing just 14 goals against and 112 saves in 1250 minutes played. Trey Ogilvie, our leading scorer, finished 48th in the country in scoring with 12 goals and 2 assists for 26 points. Twenty of the twenty-eight players scored during the 2011 campaign. Gudie Guzman was named to the Region XX All-Tournament team. As a team and coaching staff, we felt we were well on our way to building something special at Potomac State College.

Up Up and Away for Year Three!

I didn't practice the team for the last two months of the semester, November and December. One, it was a JUCO rule, and two, our boys needed a break from soccer so they could focus on academics. No one knows what it is like to be a college athlete trying to meet the academic demands and the athletic grind. It is especially difficult if you are a Division III athlete who is not receiving any financial scholarship money. They are just there for the love of the game and to secure a degree!

The only meeting scheduled was the one-hour meeting between our coaching staff and each individual athlete. We would discuss each player's goals and desires for the spring semester and the following year. Some would return as sophomores. Sophomores would move on to other colleges for academic reasons and/or to continue playing soccer. Some would have found out college was not for them, and they would join the workforce, military, or go to a trade school. Whatever their desires were, we as coaches would work to see that their needs were fulfilled. We also had each player fill out a brief evaluation of the program. You only need three questions:

- What did you like about the program?
- What did you dislike about the program?
- What changes would you make if you were the coach of Potomac State College?

In January, we started the entire program for 2012 again. We would evaluate last season and who was returning, and what our needs were for recruiting. We discussed the athletes we saw during the fall and who we still needed to evaluate. As for 2012, we were pretty well set with 13 sophomores returning. I also had made an inroad with an Australian recruiting service in 2011 through the NSCAA convention that brought me two very fine gentlemen/soccer players that I would like to recruit. Those two players were Henry Herkes from Angaston, Australia, and Nathan Main from Seton Catholic, Australia.

One of our Freshmen players, Cody Wedge, came to us from Meyersdale, Pennsylvania. Cody had a son while he was a senior at Meyersdale High School. Cody would raise Bryson while attending PSC and working towards an Associate of Arts degree in mechanical engineering, while playing soccer. Try juggling those apples as an eighteen-year-old.

Things were looking good and going well until I received a letter from my assistant, Brad Burr, stating that he was resigning. Brad said he could never find the time to tell me, so he put it in a letter. It was a very gracious resignation that stated he had other life goals he would like to focus on rather than PSC soccer. This letter warmed my heart but also punched me in the gut. I missed coaching with Brad after the spring of 2012. He was the best!

Brad planned to work through Spring 2012, including on the field maintenance. Yes, Brad did recover from last 'year's field development wounds.

In January, we joined a Procare Sportsplex Indoor Soccer League in Bedford, Pennsylvania. This required that our players travel 100 round-trip miles on Sunday nights. Not all players could play each week due to trips home on weekends. I get it and understand; however, we were able to muster enough players each week to field two teams. Procare had a great theme for their Sportsplex. 'Where The Kid in All of Us Wants To Play.' I remember this as I played in an over-50 tournament a couple of summers ago while well into my 50's. We always seemed to muster 20 "kids" over 50 years of age. One kid was over 70 years of age. Thanks, Vince Celtnieks.

I also took on some other challenges over the 2012 spring/summer. I worked with the Southern/Oakland, Maryland soccer club to train their youth coaches. Mark Sprouse, our women's soccer coach, teamed up to run soccer camps on campus at PSC, Southern High School, Oakland, Maryland; Hyndman High School, Hyndman, Pennsylvania; and Northern High School, Grantsville, Maryland.

I Have a Face for Radio

Jim Zamagais, long-time teacher, coach, and athletic director at Bishop Walsh School, was announcing boys' soccer games on WCBC radio on AM 1270. Jim asked me to join him and provide color in the fall of 2012. We worked games around my fall season. This worked very

231

well for me. Jim was announcing high school soccer, volleyball, football, and youth league baseball. Jim is a great announcer and analyst. He could make a chicken fight sound exciting.

The only thing I brought to the table was some soccer insight and a "goalllllllllllllllll" call that I could drag out for as many as two solid minutes. Sometimes it would take Jim two minutes to figure out who assisted or scored the goal. Jim would look through his binoculars and raise his hand like a conductor for me to keep dragging out the goal call until I was blue in the face! Fun! Fun! Fun!

I also wanted to thank Dave "Norman" Aydelotte, who owns and operats WCBC, for his commitment to the Cumberland, Maryland, and tri-state area for carrying all of the local sports to highlight our youth in the area.

Two very exciting events happened while recruiting that spring of 2012. We landed some very respected local players from Mountain Ridge High School, coached by Tim Nightengale. Tim has won several State Championships in the Maryland 1A classification. Tim is a great teacher and coach. He followed me after I left Beall High School back in 2001. Mountain Ridge was a new high school built on the Beall High site back in 2007. Remember, I was the first person thrown out of Mountain Ridge's new stadium. Connor Eberly, Chris Ranker, Brandon Cutter, and Jordan Cook were state champions at the Ridge in 2011 and decided to come play with Justin Winebrenner and Zach Saylor from the 2010 class.

Connor Eberly and Chris Ranker were top players in the state of Maryland. Respectively, a goalkeeper and a forward. Eberly called me to say that he and Chris had made up their minds and were coming to PSC to play soccer. I was so excited that I could not believe my ears. Connor and Chris said they were coming, but I would have to do their laundry! I was stunned by the request, and then the two broke out laughing on the conference call. They got me. They were such great finds, I probably would have given in and done their laundry. The life of a JUCO coach!!!

The other exciting news was that not only Mountain Ridge players, but also additional quality players from around the area were now flocking to PSC. Local players were taking notice, and we were getting them to come play for the Catamounts. We added Steve Holtschneider, a three-sport athlete, and Jeffrey Trautwein from Northern/Garrett, and Jacob Strawn from Hampshire High School in Romney, West Virginia.

Oh yeah, I had to replace Coach Burr. I found two proven high school coaches in their fields, respectively. Steve Amann was an assistant and head coach at Westmar High School in the late 90's through the closing of Westmar in 2006. Steve then assisted Martha Mauzy with the girls' program at Mountain Ridge from 2007 to 2011. Steve, like all good soccer coaches, wore many hats, being involved in youth coaching in the area and established the annual Senior All-Star Game held each November in the Tri-State area.

Tom Dawson became my second assistant coach. Our budget only allowed for one assistant coach, so I used our camp money to pay for

Tom's salary. Tom was a long-time friend of mine! He had coached soccer in the George's Creek area for eight years. He had coached cross country and track & field at Westmar High School in Lonaconing, Maryland. In 1998, Tom's Westmar boys' team won the 1A Maryland State Cross Country Championship.

With Conor Fungaroli returning, I made Connor Eberly a field player. He was a flat-out good athlete and could play anywhere in the field. He focused on outside midfield, and he enjoyed being on the field after playing the last couple of years between the pipes. This would also give us a solid keeper for the next year if everything fell in place following Fungaroli's sophomore departure.

With all our talent as players and a coaching staff, we were destined to have a great season in 2012. We won our first 8 games and were tenth in the JUCO Division III National Rankings. We lost our first game in a hard-fought battle at Prince George's Community College. I had always struggled against PGCC as a player and JUCO soccer coach, but felt this was our year. However, we doubled them in shots and corners and lost the game 0-1. Officiating didn't help on our away trip, but it never does in JUCO soccer. You need to have your players ready to play the game and not just in the moment. Whatever just happened in the moment, move on and play the game.

We then strung together seven wins in a row before finishing the season against our old foe, Montgomery Rockville. This was at their school; the field had a baseball infield in the corner of the field. This should never have been allowed in a college soccer setting. Too many injuries occur stepping from the grass to the infield dirt. We gave up two corner kicks for goals and lost the game 1-3. We knew the Region XX championship would have to go through MRCC. We needed to move on, only suffering a 0-1 and 1-3 loss. We finished the season 15-2.

We became the number one seed in 2012 because MRCC had not played Northern Virginia Community College in the regular season. We beat NVCC twice during the regular season. Garrett had good games against NVCC. He had a good sophomore season. Not easy being the son of the head coach. He handled himself well! I was proud of Garrett.

We had to play Anne Arundel CC in the semifinal after receiving a bye for being the number one seed in Region XX. It was nice to have the first round bye, but the tournament was at Anne Arundel CC, and our semifinal game was on their field. We worked hard that night and pulled out a 2-0 win on Thursday night. We would then travel home that night after a 9pm finish and drive another 2 and a half hours home. We practiced (light) on Friday and had to drive another 2 and a half hours back to AACC to face Montgomery Rockville at 1:00pm on Saturday. We departed our Keyser campus at 7:00 am. We just did not have the budget to stay overnight for two nights. Tough on our players.

The Region XX Championship game was quite a feat for us in our third year of the campaign, with Ray Kiddy as the head coach, two new assistant coaches, and quite a tough grinding season. Potomac State

College had just won three games the year before we started building in 2010.

Montgomery Rockville had a very good team, but we were up for the task. We received an obvious penalty kick in the first half. Steve Holtschneider was 5 for 5 on penalties this fall, and I was sure he would make his sixth. He hit the ball to the far right post, and their goalkeeper made a great save. I thought the keeper left early and pleaded our case, to no avail. We entered the second half at 0-0.

Steve Holtschneider came over to me at the half to apologize about the penalty kick. Play the game, not the moment, Steve.

"Steve, your front tooth is vertical and sticking over your lip."

He felt it, stuck it in the cavity, and went over and got a drink. We talked at halftime with the team to keep working hard so we could win the game. Steve went back in the second half and played the game not in the moment. One tough son of a gun.

The second half was back and forth until MRCC scored a nice goal from the eighteen. We fought hard to get back into the game, and MRCC played tough defense. We dominated the last ten minutes. Nathan Main just shot a bicycle kick that I had no idea how their goalkeeper tracked it, but he did. We lost the game 0-1, and MRCC celebrated like they had never been there before, which they had. MRCC went on to the 16 national tournament and lost in the championship game. That is how close and how far we had come in just three years. This is exciting stuff.

We ended the 2012 campaign at 16-3 and regular season Region XX Champions. I was named DIII Region XX Coach of the year. Chris Ranker finished his freshman season scoring 14 goals, placing 11th in goals and 30th in points among Division III players. Conor Fungaroli finished 11th in the nation in goals against (0.73) per year and 27th in save percentage (804). Trey Ogilvie of Winchester, Va, and Gudie Guzman of El Salvador via Berkeley Springs also finished nationally ranked. Ogilvie was 18th in goals (12) and 36th in points (25), and Guzman was 29th in assists (7).

I spent a lot of time recruiting. When you want half of your kids to be local, you have to see a lot of games. You also have to watch a lot of tape and be on the phone to recruit worldwide. You also have to do this part-time along with your other job as assistant principal at Allegany High School. I love this game.

First Team All-Region XX Selections were Guidie Guzman, Conor Fungaroli, Steve Holtschneider, and Second Team Justin Winebrenner. All Region XX All Tournament Selections were Justin Winebrenner, Conor Fungaroli, and Steve Holtschneider. Region XX Sophomores All-Star Game Selections were Henry Herkes, Garrett Kiddy, Nathan Main, and Jeffrey Trautwein.

The All-Star Game was our third trip to AACC. Eight hours of travel in nine days'! You have to love this game.

Can It Get Any Better?

In the spring of 2013, we did our usual: recruit, train both indoor and out, plan for summer camps with Mark Sprouse. I could not get my assistant coaches to buy into helping with summer camps. I didn't push because of the time the job consumed during the fall. Steve and Tom were good assistants from the standpoint of doing what you asked of them. I always struggled with the fact that they did not take the initiative to create and work beyond the asking. Assistant coaches need to foresee what is needed to make the program blossom. This is critical! This is coming from the worst assistant coach ever! Me!

The fall of 2013 gave way to another education adventure. The Allegany County Board of Education named me Supervisor of Physical Education and Athletics, along with serving as Assistant Principal at Allegany High School. This was going to take some more time in my day to operate these two areas. These areas would include evaluations of PE teachers and coaches, oversight of the two budgets, and preparation and execution of professional development days. Oh yeah! Why not take on more work?

The spring did bring something special to my heart and to one of our players. Cody Wedge of Meyersdale, Pennsylvania, celebrated his graduation from Potomac State College on May 12, 2013. Cody graduated with an Associate of Arts degree in mechanical engineering. He celebrated with his three-year-old son on that special day. I often think of the dedication Cody had to work so hard academically, play two years of college soccer, and raise a young son. Yes, he had assistance from his family, but this is quite a chunk of organization to pull from within. When I was his age, I was trying to figure out how to study and become a better soccer player. Now that's simple compared to what Cody Wedge accomplished. I always said the key to success is organization. You also have to add a lot of love and patience to Cody's situation.

Our recruiting that spring went well, being able to continue with some sound local talent and good returning players. We had 6 returning sophomores from last season and 16 newcomers. However, this year brought in a special Australian player, Brandon Lee from Brisbane. Brandon looked like a good player in pre-season, but not the force he would become in September and October.

We were at a pre-season exhibition game with Frostburg State University. FSU—my alma mater and where I had coached for four years—is on that long list of when was Kiddy there? We lost the exhibition game 1-3, and I was playing Brandon at midfield and on defense.

As we cleaned up our bench area at FSU, Brandon came up to me and said, "Coach Kiddy, I think I can help score for us."

After what I just witnessed, I thought my mother could score for us wearing high heels. We were god awful offensively that afternoon. I told Brandon I was going to give him a shot up front next week. Twenty-five goals later, Brandon was right. He could score for us or any other team in the JUCO universe.

I was more excited this season for our four returning sophomores, Connor Eberly, Chris Ranker, Brandon Cutter, and Caleb Goodin. They had great seasons last year, and I wanted them to finish this season well. They were good students, athletes, and gentlemen. You will not find a better group of young men. I was also excited because Gabe Kiddy, my youngest son, had decided to attend PSC. His brother Garrett departed following two solid years at PSC, and Gabe wanted to give it a try. Gabe had suffered a separated patella in his senior year of high school and had a successful surgery. I was excited to see him compete at the college level. Gabe said, "When I was being recruited, I had a recruiter in my house every night"!" True Gabe!

Gabe was slow in the back after knee surgery, but would take you down if you tried to beat him. He would foul you outside the box on a wrestling move, a take-down. The official would make the call against Gabe. I would say, "Don't do it again, Gabe." That was code for Gabe to keep the good work up!

Potomac State College went unbeaten in its first fifteen games to post a 13-0-2 record. Brandon Lee and returning Sophomore Chris Ranker teamed up for a total of 33 goals with one regular season game remaining. Connor Eberly, who was gracious enough to play the field the year before, had an outstanding season between the pipes. Connor recorded 8 shutouts during the regular season.

Bubba Showed Up

The last regular season game was against Montgomery Rockville, again! We were ranked nationally, bouncing from sixth to eighth several times during the season. However, MRCC was ranked as high as number two and was the real deal this season. We suffered a 1-3 loss, bringing us down to earth prior to the Region XX playoffs. The most goals we had given up in the regular season were 2. This loss to MRCC was the bomb under our feet. When you suffer a loss like this, you have to say, forget it, move on, next team up! Keep it simple. Everyone and every team will see Bubba out there, who is bigger, stronger, and quicker. You saw Bubba, now deal with it.

We know who we are. We had a great 14-1-2 regular season. We are solid from the goalkeeper to the front line. We are seeded second in Region XX. We regain confidence in a playoff game before facing MRCC in the Region XX Championship. One game at a time and move one.

Chris Ranker broke a scoreless silence off a corner kick against Prince George's CC at the 26-minute mark of the first half. From there, it was up to Connor Eberly, who held the Owls off the scoreboard by making eight saves in his ninth shutout of the season. Let's go face Bubba!

We traveled to meet MRCC two days later at Prince George's CC on a Saturday. Another three-hour drive after the six-hour round trip on Thursday. MRCC had a one-hour drive. Who sets these playoff sites, days, and times? Should the neutral site between number one and two in Region XX be halfway? Now that makes sense.

241

We started out slow. And I mean slow! The only ones slower than PSC were the officials. The official was not wearing glasses, probably forgot their glasses. I hate to complain about officials, so I won't. We gave up two penalty kicks and lost one of our top players, who suffered two yellow cards and was ejected from the game. The rule is that the player has to leave the facility. I had to put him on the bus with the bus driver. Fortunately, Connor Eberly stopped one of the penalty kicks, and we were only down 3-1 at the half and playing with ten players in the field. MRCC does not need these types of breaks, but they received them.

We ended up losing 1-6. It is hard to overcome the number two team in the country with ten players, and the Raptors awarded two penalty kicks. We finished the season 15-2-2 and nationally ranked 8th in the country. I was proud of our team. Brandon was named to the All-Region XX First team and also to the Region XX All-Region XX Tournament Team. Lee finished third in the NJCAA Division III scoring race, scoring 25 goals and six assists.

Connor Eberly was named to the Region XX All-Tournament Team and to the Second Team All-Region. He recorded nine shutouts in 19 games for the Catamounts. Connor served as one of four captains and was listed in the 'Top Twenty' Goalkeepers in four different goalkeeping areas in the country.

Chris Ranker was named to the Region XX Second Team All-Region XX, scoring 12 goals and 6 assists. This was the second consecutive year that he has scored 12 goals.

Brandon Cutter was named to the Region XX Second Team All-Region XX. He led our defense, allowing only 20 goals during the season. You have a chance of never losing a game with Brandon in the back. He only has one speed: fast and aggressive.

Caleb Goodin was named to the Region XX All-Tournament Team. Caleb did it all for us this year, including scoring a goal coming out of the back against MRCC in the Region Tournament.

Jerad Fike (freshman) was named to the All-Region Second Team as a midfielder. Fike finished the season with three goals and one assist. He was our assassin, known for his hard-nosed defense.

Wow! What a season. Our sophomores finished with a 31-5-2 record.

Could This Be the Roller Coaster Year?

We started in August with dorm check-in, meetings, and our first week of practices. We had one week to prepare for two scrimmages with Shenandoah University and Patrick Henry College. We had some bright new commers in Alec Sproul from Umina, Australia, Austin Parker from Fort Hill High School, and Patrick Kimble from Mountain Ridge,

We had 21 players, and the preseason went well. The boys were very competitive, and we were opening our new turf field. These were exciting times for Potomac State College Soccer for both the men's and women's soccer programs.

We started out 4-0 before a weekend road trip to Mercyhurst Northeast in Pennsylvania and then onto Corning Community College in New York. This was our first trip for PSC, where we stayed overnight. The guys were excited because we had two exciting games, plus we were traveling with the women's team. What could go wrong?

When we arrived to play Mercyhurst Northeast, they were warming up! I could tell that with some thirty players and an international roster, we would be in for a tough game. We played a back-and-forth first half with Patrick Kimble hitting a hard shot near the eighteen-yard box with one minute to go. The problem was that Patrick suffered a season-ending knee injury on the play. This was a tough blow for our team. You could tell the team felt bad for Pat, and I did, too. However, I did feel good about our team unity and chemistry when I saw how bad they felt for Pat Kimble. This was the kind of culture I wanted for Potomac State College Men's soccer.

We went on to win the game over Mercyhurst Northeast 2-0. One of our best wins in my five years at PSC. We went on to Corning C.C. the next day. We arrived early and warmed up, but you could tell we had tired legs from the game prior. Corning had struggled prior to our arrival, going 0-5 at the start of the season. We matched that struggle with a 1-1 halftime score. Alec Sproule had done an excellent job in the goal, but we just did not have the legs. Because of their lack of confidence, we squeezed out a 3-1 victory and ended our long weekend trip with a 6-0 start to the season.

We won the next two unevenly matched games against Blue Ridge C.C. and Lord Fairfax C.C.! We are 8-0. Alec Sproul and our defense have only given up 4 goals in eight games. Next up, Northern Virginia C.C., which was 0-6. A trap game it was. We played on the original Washington Redskin practice field back in the 1960's. The turf was beat up, and we struggled the entire game. NOVA beat us 1-0 and ended our eight-game winning streak.

Next up was a home game against Anne Arundel Community College. They always have a competitive team, with Annapolis being a hotbed for Maryland soccer. I felt good about the game since we were back at home. It was a battle, and with 20 seconds to go in regulation, Austin Parker received his second yellow card of the game, and we entered overtime with ten players. Austin Parker is one of those defenders you do not want to face. He was a pitbull in the box. AACC coaches had talked and chatted the entire game with the officials about his physical play that they announced as dirty. He was a great player. If I could have Austin Parker and Steve Holtschneider from the 2011-12 team, I would go to battle against any level of college soccer in NCAA or JUCO.

Thirty seconds into overtime, AACC was awarded a corner kick. We needed Austin in the six-yard box on corners and did not have him. They scored on a header that would not have happened if Parker were in the game. I assigned him to the middle of six, and all air balls were his. When I arrived in the locker room, tough man Austin Parker was crying. He did not lose the game by not being in the game. We lost the game because we relied on one player in a team sport. I did like Austin's character and that he could show emotion to and for his team.

Brandon Lee suffered an ankle injury and was out for the next six games. We have lost Patrick Kimble for the season, and we were scrambling from the beginning of every kickoff for the remainder of the season. We had lost our confidence at this point of the season, finishing 3-5 during the remainder of the regular season.

When Brandon Lee injured his ankle, he was leading all Divisions of JUCO soccer with 25 goals and six assists. Thirty goals was the top scorer in JUCO that year. Had Brandon Lee been healthy, he would have topped that score and would have been a JUCO player of the year. Our team and coaches awaited Brandon's return during the season, but it was too late; we were spiraling out of control.

Brandon Lee had suffered an injury that was devastating to him and our team. I always feel it is best to listen to the athlete and the athletic trainers before the athletes return. I can ask for the athlete back immediately for the team. But as a coach, you always have to think of the future of the players' health. He/she will play and have to deal with the injury long after you are the coach.

We finished the regular season 11-7. Those sophomores were a good group and fun. I will always remember those sophomores: Rose Lopez, Jerad Fike, Brandon Lee, Eric Szymanski, Matt Tice, Brandon Jones, Beck Sherrard, Jacob Williams, Jake Benford, and my youngest son, Gabe Kiddy.

We lost in the first round of the Region XX playoffs. Our first season in three years that we were not in the Region XX final. You could say it was a rollercoaster of a season. But I felt we were plummeting as a program. Your program always has to be changing and evolving with the times, and we were not as a coaching staff. You have to have team chemistry as a coaching staff. We needed change, and it had to start with me.

We had established a program that had set the school record at fifteen wins. In 2014, we had dropped to eleven wins. Any year your win column is in double-digits, you feel good.

In the individual awards that year, Brandon Lee was named First Team JUCO All-American (not bad for an Australian). Brandon had scored fifty goals in two years, and eleven of his goals were game winners. Brandon was also named All-Region XX First Team. Jerad Fike was named to the All-Region XX second team.

Nothing To Be Proud About!

As usual, we carried on with spring training, games, weight training, and recruiting. I felt the program needed a boost or a change. This year, we decided to add our own spring tournament along with a youth camp coached by our players. It was time to give the lads an opportunity to have some leadership and to coach youth. This should have happened sooner in our program instead of year six. Most of the camps were in the summer when Mark Sprouse, Donnie Amman, and I were available. The players were home for the summer and not available for this experience.

247

We ran a youth clinic in the morning for ages 4-13! The boys' and girls' clinic focused solely on the fundamentals of the game through creative teaching exercises and games that kept the players' interest and guaranteed they would have fun. The clinic run by our players gave the campers an opportunity to develop a solid foundation that will help them at every level of the game. Goalkeepers received individual training.

Following the camp, we had a 7-aside Tournament for the campers to stay and observe. We had two PSC Alumni teams: Frederick CC, WVU Club, and Allegany College of Maryland. Each team was guaranteed three games, and then four teams played in the semi's and two in the finals. The day went well, but my assistants could not help with the day because of other commitments.

Another commitment for my assistants was becoming a habit, and it gave me an additional workload. Actually, these other commitments and my full-time job for the Allegany County Board of Education were grinding on me. I still had a family with three sons in college. I created this problem by taking all these responsibilities on myself. I had no one to blame but Ray Kiddy.

Summer came. We sent the returnees home with their workouts, and we finished with the sophomore meetings to set them on their way to the great beyond. During the summer, I knew we needed some change. I brought the best information I could out of our Winter NSCAA convention in Philly and wanted to freshen things up. Unfortunately, we needed more than this!

Our schedule for the fall of 2015 was as tough as ever. We would open with our Labor Day weekend tournament, including Suffolk CC, the 2014 defending Division II runner-up. We only had one snooze game on our schedule along with the Region XX opponents, who all had become very competitive over the past five years.

I hired Conner Eberly and Caleb Goodin, two graduated players, for us who wanted a taste of coaching. These were in addition to the 2 assistant coaches already in place. I thought this might help with our other coaches having many other outside commitments.

We beat the WVU Club team in our opening tournament and then lost to Suffolk CC, 1-3, in a hard-fought game. With ten minutes to go in the game, we were down 2-1 and knocking on their door. Suffolk got a breakaway with three minutes to go in the game. They knocked one home, and we suffered our first loss of 2015.

Alec Sproul, our sophomore goalkeeper from Australia, was having a great season, but the rest of us were inconsistent. Alec was demanding of his teammates, loud in his control of the team, and he had great keeper skills. I just wish we could have responded and been more supportive of Alec.

During one of our last games of the season, Alec suffered a back injury and was helicoptered out of our stadium and sent to Ruby Memorial Hospital in Morgantown, West Virginia. We lost Alec for the playoffs.

We finished the season 8-6 and finished in 6th place in Region XX. This was quite a drop for us. We lost to Anne Arundel in the quarterfinals and completed the season 8-7. Prior to the finish of the season, I fired one coach to split up the two four-year coaches. I needed to make a change. They were no longer helping our situation. Not something I am proud of, but I knew it was necessary. Know that when you hire someone, you may have to fire them one day.

Two high notes of the season were that Alec Sproul was named First Team JUCO All-American and Jacob Williams was named Academic All-American. This was a well-deserved award for a goalkeeper who played on a team that had finished the 2015 season 8-7. This was an award that was recognized by our Region XX coaches, who respected all aspects of Alec's goalkeeping game.

Jacob William was a steady player for us, and he gave me some advice and insight into the team during the season. It is always good when your players are smarter than you. Thanks, Jacob!

Both Alec and Jacob are engineers today!

Departure!

Following the 2015 fall season, I let Shawn White, our Athletic Director, know that I would be leaving Potomac State College. I would continue the winter, spring, and fall 2016 season. I wanted to give Shawn plenty of time to find a good replacement. I did not want to let the team know until the completion of the 2016 fall season. I did not want anything to disrupt recruiting or winter and spring workouts prior to the fall of 2016.

I also let the Allegany County Board of Education know I would be retiring, too. In January of 2016, prior to our coaching trip to Philadelphia, I took the Bishop Walsh Athletic Director position on a part-time basis until June of 2016. At that time, I would become the full-time Dean of Students and Athletic Director. I will have come full circle. I began at Bishop Walsh teaching and coaching from 1978 to 1985, and would return. I knew that recruiting athletes and students for BW would interfere with recruiting at Potomac State College.

At the NSCAA convention, we had taken Alec Sproul and Jacob Williams to receive their All-American Awards. It was an exciting time for our coaching staff. We attended our Australian recruiting service party on Saturday night of the convention. This party was one of the nicest celebrations I attended at any convention. A lot was changing in my life at this point, with the departure and acceptance of new adventures.

Alec Sproul and Brandon Lee accepted athletic scholarships to the University of Texas, Permian Basin. They would continue their degrees in engineering while fulfilling their dreams of playing soccer at a high level. Brandon and Alec had worked so hard to reach their goals. They would soon turn the UTPB soccer program around while earning their Engineering degrees. I was so proud of both gentlemen.

Following the convention, we got back to work, recruiting and working out the returnees. I was now AD at Walsh and adding those duties until I retired as Assistant Principal, and supervisor of PE and Athletics. What a load!

Twenty-eight players participated in spring workouts. I felt good about our recruiting class. Steve Amman, my remaining assistant for 2016, decided his work at Mead Westvaco would not allow him to coach in the fall. I appreciated his decision when he let me know in July 2016. This was a little late to find an assistant, so I asked Connor Eberly if he could return for the fall season. Connor was studying at Frostburg University and said he could assist with practices and home games, but could not travel to away games. I totally understood, and we shook hands. I would be the only one carrying the load on away games. Not much new here since I had assistants who at one time could not even hand out sandwiches on road trips. Move on, Ray!

We opened up the season with a 0-1 loss in overtime to Washington Adventist College. This was another back-and-forth battle. Jacob Dale, our freshman back from Bishop Walsh School, played an outstanding game on defense and helped us stay in the game. He had to defend a monster of a player for ninety minutes. They hit a shot just outshot the eighteen in overtime. We are now 0-1. They are a four-year institution.

Our Labor Day Tournament weekend was next. I invited Patrick Henry Community College. They were the prior JUCO Division I runner-up in 2015. We played with Division III runner-up last year (Suffolk CC), suffering a tough 1-3 loss. Why not?

In our first game on the weekend, we lost to WVU Club 0-2. Then the bomb was dropped. Five of our starting players told me prior to the weekend that they would not be available for the second game against PHCC. They all had jobs that required them to work part of Labor Day weekend. You know my philosophy: next man up. This is JUCO soccer at its finest.

During warmups, PHCC had thirty-eight players, with eighteen of them being international. I knew we would be in for a wild game. They scored five goals in the first ten minutes of the game. We never recovered. We suffered a 0-16 loss. My biggest loss in my thirty-six years. My biggest win ever was a 16-0 high school victory when I was at Beall High School. The score was fitting! I worried about recovering as a team mentally, following the weekend. I stressed that due to our undermanned lineup, we had to get this out of our heads and move on to the next team. We are now 0-3! Ouch. I had never lost the first three games in my career since Catonsville Community College back in 1986. That was 24 teams ago.

Following the game, Lori and I and other friends drove to Rochester, New York, to attend a friend's daughter's' wedding. Two years ago, the family lost their teenage daughter. It was important that we attended. When we returned, we learned that another friend had lost a son in a drowning accident. Bad timing and the hits just keep coming. A loss in a game is just a loss. A loss of life, there is no recovery.

We never recovered from the slow start. For the second year in a row, we were the sixth seed in the playoffs and suffered a first-round loss to Anne Arundel. We completed the season with a 5-9 record. Tyler Sisler led us in scoring and was named All-Region XX Second Team, and Rhys Fing, another Australian player, was All-Region XX Honorable Mention.

I never wanted what we had built in seven years at PSC to finish the way it did in 2016. No one did! Sometimes you work so hard you do not see a season coming like the past fall. I was the one to blame. I had too many balls in the air to juggle, and they all came crashing down. The players in 2016 deserved better than they received! Sorry guys!

Chapter 24: Recovery

"Healing does not rest in the hands of a selected few but in the hands of every human being"."

-Blair Justice

When I became the principal of Bishop Walsh School, the Archdiocese of Baltimore leaders told me I had six months to turn enrollment numbers and our financial situation around. They said I have the toughest job right now in their entire organization.

When you have a tough job to accomplish, think big!

Having great mentors as a sounding board is important in decision-making.

Award voting in athletics is very political.

During the summer of 2018, I had a guidance counselor and a head basketball coach opening. As Principal, I needed to fill those positions, and the basketball piece was important to our school community since we were the host school to one of the most popular national basketball tournaments on the planet. The ACIT (Alhambra Catholic Invitational Tournament) was established some 75 years ago and hosted some of the best Catholic Schools in the United States and Canada.

With the help of Brian Mullaney, former student, athletic director, and alum, we found a great gentleman by the name of Dan Prete. When

I say gentleman, I mean in every aspect of the word. Dan had coached high school ball at Montrose Christian, St Andrew's Episcopal, and St. James. When I met Dan, he had some 8 players associated with the NBA in a player capacity or coaching. I hired Dan as my Guidance Counselor and Head Basketball Coach at BW. A win/win for everyone.

Brian Mullaney, with the help of many others, established a dormitory in Cumberland to house our new basketball team that Dan brought with him. Brian was in Ocean City, Maryland, making a trip to bring back extra-large beds for our b-ball team that was going to need to sleep 6'7-7'0 foot athletes. While making a fast food stop, a man asked Brian what he was doing. He explained our new endeavor with our small school in Cumberland, Maryland.

The man said, "I have a niece in Honduras that I would like to get to the States. Do you have girls' soccer?"

Brian said, "We sure do," and the rest is history!

Brian passed the man's information on to me, and we worked on getting his niece to Bishop Walsh. Ale Puerto was the niece's name, and she came towards the end of September 2018 to attend BW and play for our soccer team. Ale assisted in turning our soccer program around. She is now captain of the Honduras National Soccer Team. WOW! Can this all be happening to our small school on the mountain, Bishop Walsh?

August was upon us, and it was my second year as the head soccer coach following the 2017 season to forget. I had ordered new uniforms for the ladies for the 2018 season. We needed a new look, and our Athletic Director, Carl Watson, agreed. Anything that would give us a fresh start following a 3-12 season last season. I had Score Sports out of California do the design for our new uniforms with a cross on the sleeve. Our softball team had used this design prior to our soccer girls'! I liked the look, so we did the same because we can. It is great at a private catholic school to give praise and recognition to God and the Catholic religion. It not only says something about us but also demonstrates to others what we are all about. We are not special, but we are under watchful eyes.

Sister Phyllis McNally was a former principal at Bishop Walsh School. She was a guidance counselor at Bishop Walsh when I started at Walsh back in the late 70's. Sister Phyllis was always a shoulder to lean on and bounce ideas off during my thirteen years at Bishop Walsh. I can never thank her enough for being a sounding board throughout my educational career. She was our biggest cheerleader during the Dan Prete era for the Spartans.

Our soccer preseason went well, splitting with Rockwood and Spring Mills. Of our seventeen players, ten were seniors. The seniors were our captains, and they rotated three each game to wear the arm bands. All of the seniors showed great leadership. In the past, I have told you that when you have double-digit seniors, you are in the money. This proved to be true. We played 500 ball during the first half of the season, being led by Erin Langan, Lauren Mathews, and Sarah Wharton. Miriam Klosterman had recorded five shutouts. However, when Ale Puerto

257

arrived halfway through the season, things started looking better. Her touch and skill level were what we needed. She gave another scoring punch, giving us six goals, but also was great at spraying the ball around and led us in assists with five. We finished 2-2 in the city matches and completed the season with an overall 11-8 season.

Senior Rosie Duncan was named Defensive Player of the Year for the Area, along with first-team Erin Langan. Lauren Mathews was second team, while Sarah Wharton was Honorable Mention. Bella Biancone joined the above Allstars as being named All City.

In 2015, when I became Athletic Director at Bishop Walsh, I started the Small School Mountain Athletic Conference (SSMAC). I wanted BW to have a level playing field with small schools to give all involved recognition. This conference consisted of BW, Calvary Christian Academy, Hancock, Hope for Hyndman, Light House Christian Academy, Northern (Garrett), and Trinity Christian School. This was the third conference, dating back to the 1979 Bi-State Soccer League and the 2005 Appalachian Mountain Athletic Conference (AMAC), in which I had been a leader in organizing. Duncan, Langan, and Wharton were named to the All SMACC All-Stars. This was a turning point season for BW after a dismal 4-10-2 in 2016 and our season to forget, a 3-12 mark. Organizing a conference is good, rewarding work because all those Athletic Directors involved are positive and want the best for their student athletes. Following the first year of the organization is when the nuts and bolts become loose. Look out then!

Recovery to Rebound

After a long and hard soul-searching summer, I decided to let the Archdiocese of Baltimore and the Bishop Walsh community know I would be retiring at the end of the 2019-2020 school year. This would give everyone involved plenty of time to find my replacement. I felt that I had completed many things in my short four years of principalship and had enough energy to give one more year. William E. Lori, Archbishop of Baltimore, wrote me a grateful letter for my leadership and solicitude for the students and staff of Bishop Walsh.

Onto soccer because it is August 2019. After graduating, half of our team, Donnie, and I were very optimistic because of the building of enrollment at Bishop Walsh. We had several good athletes transfer into BW and had an outstanding Freshman and Sophomore class. Our school had grown from 64 high school students to 115. Our total enrollment for the 2019-2020 school year was 415. Not bad for a k-12 catholic school these days.

No Goalkeeper

The problem our squad had was that Miriam Klosterman had graduated, and we did not have a true goalkeeper. Miriam was steady, strong, and made good decisions. We needed to take a good athlete and make them into a goalkeeper. I put that responsibility on Donnie, since he had worked with Miriam the past two seasons. We decided to split responsibilities in half between Ale Puerto and Sarah Wharton. Both were very good athletes. Ale came to us from Honduras speaking four English words, and in one year at BW, she was speaking the English language better than yours truly. The problem was that we also needed her in the field. Sarah Wharton became the second-half goalie in all games.

Sarah was athletic and strong in the air. The problem was that she had never played the position prior. Now that I mention it, when Sarah came to us as a freshman, she had never played soccer before. In Middle School, she played youth football on her team as a linebacker and running back. That tells you how strong Sarah would be in the goal.

Both girls, Ale and Sarah, grew with the position. They actually became very steady. Ale provided 22 goals scored and five assists while only playing forty minutes a game. Sarah was a steady midfielder and contributed all around in any position we needed her when not playing in the goal.

We opened the preseason, splitting again with Spring Mills and Rockwood. The only difference was that we were beating Rockwood 6-0 in a scrimmage when they asked for the mercy rule to end the game early. There was a big difference when they dominated us two years ago. Donnie and I knew we were coaching a special team.

We played steadily the entire season as a team. We only lost three games to Hampshire, Mercersburg, and Mountain Ridge. Two of the games were in area play, so we finished third in the area standings. Just two years ago, we were dead last in the ten-team race. We finished the season with a very respectable 12-3 record and were SSMAC champions. Somehow, Ale was not the offensive player of the year, scoring 22 goals, while the girl who won that award had only 8 goals. Award voting can become very political.

Ale Puerto finished her last two years at Bishop Walsh and received an NCAA Division II soccer scholarship to play at Fairmont State University. She was a two-year starter at Fairmont. Being named to the United Soccer Coaches All-Atlantic Region second team, 2022 All-MEC (Mountain West East Conference) Second Team, and 2022 MEC All-Tournament Team as a freshman. Ale was also named to the All-MEC Team as a Freshman. Following her Second year at FSU, she went into the transfer portal and was offered a soccer scholarship to the NCAA Division I University of New Mexico Lobos. Ale is currently playing at UNM and has recently been named captain of the Honduras Women's National Soccer Team. Not bad for a girl who was recruited from a fast-food chain in Ocean City, Maryland!

Ale, Shianna Cromwell, and Lexi Appel were named All-Area First Team. Ella Squires and Sara Wharton were named to the Second Team. Jen Witt was an Honorable Mention.

Witt, Cathy Cessna and Jordan Marini were named All Bi-State, while Ella Squires was All SSMAC MVP, All Academic Lydia Mathews and Best Goalkeeper Award went to Sarah Wharton.

This was quite a ride in three years for the girls' soccer team at BW and for Donnie and me. Donnie and I are good friends, and we both talk about those three years with joy and exhaustion.

In 2020, I retired as the Principal of Bishop Walsh School and the Head Girls Soccer Coach. This completed thirteen years total at BW as a teacher, coach, Assistant Athletic Director, Athletic Director, Dean of Students, and Principal. My best years in education were spent at Bishop Walsh. In March of 2020, the Archdiocese of Baltimore shut down Bishop Walsh due to the COVID-19 restrictions. We went online for education to close out the school year. We had an outdoor graduation at the end of the school year. I departed Bishop Walsh with my head high! I received many letters of congratulations from well-wishers and alumni. I did my best!

Chapter 25: The Union

"It's what you learn after you know it all that counts."

-John Wooden

A great boss makes you feel important and needed.

In March 2021, I was hired by Anthony Flores, Youth Technical Director for the Philadelphia Union (Major League Soccer). I was hired as a youth soccer coach. My job would be to coach camps, events, and club practices for players ages 6-16. The youth coaches could also evaluate players and make recommendations for players to try out for the Philadelphia Union Academy. Anthony Flores was a great boss! He made you feel like you were important and the Union needed you. This was a great opportunity for me at this point in my career.

The Union provided professional training for all of its youth coaches. Training was provided by Anthony and other Union coaches such as Sheldon Philips. The training included: recognizing and reporting misconduct, minor athlete safety acknowledgement, First Aid, Safety and CPR, and soccer training appropriate for each age group. They made sure you were providing top-level training for their youth. We would be assigned to work summer camps, fall and spring training for clubs, and winter holiday camps.

The camps, events, and practice training of the youth were very organized. Most camps ran from Monday through Thursday for three hours. On Friday, before your camp, you would receive a list of athletes you would be working with, including their age, sex, and any health precautions you needed to be aware of. You would also receive a lesson plan for your age group; this group was usually between 8 and 12 individuals. A great number to train! Lesson plans included small-sided games, activities, soccer techniques and strategies, and a small tournament at the end to provide good competition. The ball was always rolling, and the lads had a great soccer experience, including fun. The recommendation I would make to any parent would be to get their children involved with the Union camp. If you are a young coach, do not miss this coaching opportunity if you can coach and want to learn and grow.

The Plumber Must Provide His Own Tools

The Philadelphia Union took great care of their coaches. Training would take place at Union headquarters in Chester. PA or indoor facilities during colder weather around the Philadelphia area. They provided top-notch training, professional coaching apparel, and always had great leadership at each camp to make sure this was organized and safe for everyone involved.

My first year working for the Union, they provided mileage, as you provided your own transportation to all camps and training. The Union also invited the coaches to Union games and had tailgates for us. This was fun and made you feel you were part of the professional organization. You also had to provide your own equipment, such as cones, portable goals, balls, and pinnies. This was the only drawback I saw! The Union philosophy was that the plumber had to provide their own tools. I didn't mind because I had collected a lot over my 40-odd years of coaching, but I worried about the younger coaches who were just getting started.

In my second year, the Philadelphia Union Youth made some changes. Anthony Flores was promoted to Union U17 head coach, and Phil Griffiths became our new Youth Technical Director. Phil had been with the Union, working with the Academy training, and was well qualified for this move. Phil had the vision of each youth coach earning a Class C-level license or the United States Soccer Coaches Association National Diploma. This is a great move to make sure youth coaches are growing and learning in their trade. I had the National Diploma from the USSCA and applauded Phil's move in this direction. Phil was open to learning from you and what changes or input you could include. The Union also gave each youth coach a $10 an hour pay raise, but took away the mileage for transportation. I made $43 an hour for camps and $60 an hour for club training. I understood the move on transportation because I lived over two hours away from most of the Union work, and I was making a killing on mileage. I covered camps for the Union in Delaware, Pennsylvania, and New Jersey. There were some camps in NJ. I would take the Cape May Ferry and drive another hour and a half to a camp. The hourly rate was the most I had made during my coaching career, and the Union was good for their word and worked me 8-20 hours a month. A great part-time gig!

Working for the Philadelphia Union was a wonderful experience. I left the Union in December of 2023. I had decided to leave the Union and Lake Forest High School around the same time. Forty-two years of soccer had been a great run, but my time needed to be spent with my wife, Lori, of 38 years, and our three sons, their wives, and our four grandchildren. No regrets, and I had fun in soccer, no matter what road I traveled.

Chapter 26: Finale Two

"I care, but I'm done trying."

-Ray Kiddy

My wife says you know when it is time to retire. It is easy, you just do not fit in anymore!

Sometimes in a game, you have to make a stand, no matter what trouble it may cause.

Today is your day when you have worked smart and hard.

If I mispronounce your name or your name is misspelled on your certificate, get over it; that is part of life!

As I write this final season recap of 2023, I have COVID and cannot attend the fall awards ceremony tonight for Lake Forest High School in Felton, Delaware. I saw an advertisement for a head boys' soccer coach at Lake Forest High School on the Delaware Education Jobs site. It intrigued me because I was working for the Philadelphia Union Youth Coaches, but was missing the competitive drive of drilling, training, and putting the pieces of the puzzle together to be competitive. I applied for and received the job. The school was 35 miles from home, but about a fifty-minute drive from my home in Millsboro, Delaware. This would be the fourth state I would coach in, and I was also excited about that challenge. Questions plagued my mind. Could I still put a team together again? Did I still have the drive at age 66? Did I have the stamina to build another program?

Lake Forest High School had an enrollment of about 900 students. It was more of an agriculture and tech school, so it did not have a history of success in boys' soccer. I also learned what nice, hardworking student-athletes the soccer program currently had. The program was only thirty-three players strong, but they had a tremendous work ethic. The work ethnic was surprising because their success rate as a school had only been 58 games in the past 208 games. Wow! We had our work cut out for us. As President Lyndon B. Johnson said, "Yesterday is not ours to recover, but tomorrow is ours to win or lose."

I began by hiring Zach Hearn, a twenty-six-year-old assistant, who turned out to be a tremendous coach. Zach was also the program director of DE Turf in Frederica, Delaware. This is an outdoor sports facility with many soccer/lacrosse fields. Our Lake Forest Team enrolled in the spring season at DE Turf to get a start for Zach and me, and to get us acquainted with the players. We faced other local teams from grades 9-12. We finished the spring season, 4-5-3! Not a bad start, and we were in every game except the eleventh game when Caesar Rodney smoked us 7-0. We decided as a group then that we would not be in that type of game again, going into the fall season. The boys were good to their word!

We started out with a very tough scrimmage schedule. We beat Odessa 2-1, and lost the next two scrimmages to Maryland schools in

Kent County and Queen Anne's. Both of those games were 0-1 losses, but both of those teams were much better than us. We played our usual no-quit game to hang in both of those scrimmages. August in Felton, Delaware, is hot and muggy. We practiced five days a week from 9:00 to 11:00 on a turf field. We also had two Bermuda grass fields.

The facilities were excellent, college-like. Everything was available at Lake Forest High School to work on building a program. This area was mostly an agricultural area, which led to a great work ethic. Their great work ethic on the farms did not extend to practices on weekends. However, soccer ability or knowledge was lacking and required. Zach and I threw at them every bit of soccer drill activity, ball touches, and knowledge we could over the next seven months. Could we finally have a winning record and make the playoffs? Lake Forest had not made the playoffs since 1989, that's 34 years!

Only One Goalkeeper

As I noted earlier, we had 33 players out to make up a varsity and junior varsity team. The real challenge was that there was only one goalkeeper in the bunch. Yes, one! Not one other player wanted to volunteer to even go into the goal. So, the one keeper was a sophomore with decent skill and knowledge, but had a ton of courage and heart. This will work for the varsity, but we chose two other athletes to back him up! The junior varsity rotated players in the goal until we settled on one particular person who actually learned to like the position.

269

We opened the season with two tough one-goal losses to our arch-rival, Milford and Polytech High Schools. This was a fear of ours, to start out slow. I also made a move before the season to go with North Delaware officials. In the past, our school used the South officials. I just did my research and found out that North trained their officials frequently and allowed the coaches to evaluate them after each game online through Arbiter (an online tracking system for teams' officials).

I was sold on the North over the South officials, but knew in the back of my mind that we would not get a fair shake from South officials when we were on the road. This would occur three games on the road, and boy, was I right. Our next game after the 0-2 start was at Woodbridge High School. We played pretty well, outshot Woodbridge 24-6, but ended up with a 1-1 tie. This was caused by our 18-4 fouls, with poor officiating, two penalty kicks that were not called in our favor and Woodbridge High School's assistance of the South officials. Both Zach and I received a yellow card, and that was with great restraint on our part. Ok, we are now 0-2-1.

I looked at last year's stats, where we gave up 29 goals and scored 21! I used the incentive of these stats to motivate our guys to reverse the for and against goals that would lead to a winning season. Thus far, we had scored 4 goals and given up 6! This seemed like a realistic challenge for us! We won the next two games against Laurel and Red Lion High Schools. A step up, and we are now 2-2-1 and ranked 13th in the state's Division 2. Finally, the progress and our hard work were paying off. Could this be a turnaround for the program?

Second Red Card in My Coaching Career

I received a red card from a South official after the game because I thought there would not be another chance to voice my opinion on how he screwed my boys over two games. I sat out the 11th game of the season for the red card issued, and our boys played a tough Sussex Central to a 0-2 loss. We parked the bus (played strictly defense) in this loss and gave up 2 goals in the final 16 minutes. Sussex Central finished the season with a respectable 10-2-3. I think the boys were proud that their coach stood up for them to get the red card! I think! This was my second red card in my coaching career. Sometimes, you just need to make a stand and look for trouble. No regrets here!

We then lost 8 out of the next 9 games. We worked hard to stay in games against teams that were better than us. The energy was there, but not the results: 0-3, 2-3, 0-1, 0-3, 0-2, 0-2, 1-4, and 0-4. The last 0-4 result was our senior night against a good Indian River team that could have run it up higher than the 4-goal deficit. During this losing stretch, my energy and drive for soccer were waning. My preparation was dwindling, and I could see that this was my last season to coach! They say you know when it is time, and it was definitely time. I felt bad for our seniors.

The only highlight was that the Junior Varsity team finished with a 4-4-3 record. Yea! Our last game was against ASPIRA High School, which had won 8 games in a row at one point. We had them at home and went into halftime spirited with a 0-0 score. Could we win this last game? We scored two nice goals in the second half to win 2-0. This win gave us an overall 4-10-1 record, no winning season and no playoffs again! We ended up scoring 23 goals and giving 28, just enough to show a little improvement. Zach said after the last game that we taught our boys to play soccer, did not get the results, but somehow taught them to play soccer. He was right, but it was a lot of hard work and not enough of a payday to continue coaching soccer for me. It was over for me after 42 years, and I resigned just after the first of January in 2024. It may seem like it came to a screeching halt, but the flame was dwindling over that 8 of 9 game losing streak.

Senior Night

"To our senior soccer players of Lake Forest High School. You started this year having to adjust to a new coaching staff, and you adjusted well. Then, two of your senior teammates had preseason injuries that eliminated them from play for 95% of the regular season. You fought through all of this to keep the Lake Forest High School soccer team in every game, giving us a chance to win. Today is your day, and today will be no different.

Today is not the end of the season but the beginning of a successful life because you have endured so much during the 2023 campaign. Congratulations to our senior soccer players.

Lake Forest worked hard during the 2023 campaign, but we were just up against a long history of not knowing how to win and trying to learn the game of soccer in between sweat and tears. Two of our eight seniors suffered season-ending injuries during the preseason. These two would have been starters or logged a lot of minutes. They were missed and did return for senior night. We were led by some good athletes such as Talan Gerardi (All Conference 1st team), Jackson Starkey (All Conference 2nd team), and Nurrideen Ahmad-Statts (All Conference Honorable Mention).

As I said, I am typing as I miss my last athletic awards night because of illness, but I am not sad. These nights of awards are way too often, too many gifts for something not earned. As the band director at Allegany High School said at every band awards assembly, "and now for the parade of certificates, if I mispronounce your name or your name is misspelled on your certificate, get over it, that is part of life!

Author's Note

This book could be written by any youth, high school, or college coach who has dedicated their entire life to working with our youth and young adults. I am dedicating this book to all those women and men who devoted their lives to encouraging those who needed them in sport. Thank you for sharing my dream to be an American Soccer Coach.

Remember all of the times the ball almost went in, the bus broke down, you said the right thing, the parents supported you, the official blew the call, a players parent died at too young of an age, the ball did go in, you carried an injured player off the field and you barely made it to the bench before you dropped her, when the player did not follow your instruction, your spouse had enough of soccer, your own child did not want to play soccer, the weather cancelled the game, and when you thought you would make a better insurance sales person than coach.

Thank you for doing what you do!

Keep Coaching!

America needs you!

Appendix

Dr. Raymond Alan Kiddy - Overall Coaching Record

Year	School/Team	Sport	Record	Notes
—	—	**Soccer Coaching Record**	**344-208-25**	
1980	Bishop Walsh	Girls Track and Field	18-9	
1981	Bishop Walsh	Girls Track and Field	25-3	
1982	Bishop Walsh	Girls Track and Field	22-3	
1983	Bishop Walsh	Girls Track and Field	22-5	
1984	Bishop Walsh	Girls Track and Field	8-11	
—	—	**Track and Field Coaching Record**	**95-31**	
1988	College of Notre Dame	Women's Tennis	15-11	
1991	Allegany	Girls' Cross Country Champion	13-11	Michelle Barrett – Maryland State Champion 2A
1991	Allegany	Girls Cross Country	—	Team incomplete with four runners

1992	Allegany	Girls Basketball	18-6	WMIL Co-Champions & City Champions
1993	Fort Hill	Girls Basketball	10-12	
1994	Fort Hill	Girls Basketball	14-12	
—	—	**Basketball Coaching Record**	**42-30**	
1995	Frostburg State University	Softball	16-14	
—	—	**Overall Coaching Record**	**486-217-8**	

Ray Kiddy Soccer Coaching By Year!

Years	School / Team	Level / Gender	Duration
1978–1984	Bishop Walsh	Boys Soccer	7 years
1985	Indiana University of Pennsylvania	—	1 year
1986	Catonsville Community College	—	1 year
1987	College of Notre Dame	—	1 year
1990	Frostburg State University	Men's Soccer	1 year
1992–1993	Fort Hill High School	—	2 years
1994–1996	Frostburg State University	Women's Soccer	3 years
1997	Allegany High School	—	1 year

Year	School		Record
1998–1999	Mount Savage High School	—	2 years
2000–2001	Beall High School	—	2 years
2002–2005	Cumberland YMCA Travel	—	4 years
2006–2007	Allegany College of Maryland	—	2 years
2008–2009	Allegany High School	—	2 years
2010–2016	Potomac State College	—	7 years
2017–2019	Bishop Walsh	Girls Soccer	3 years
2022–2023	Philadelphia Union Youth Coach	—	2 years
2023	Lake Forest High School	—	1 year
Total	—	—	**42 years**

Dr. Raymond Alan Kiddy - Overall Soccer Coaching Record

Year	School / Team	Gender / Level	Record
1978	Bishop Walsh High School	Boys	4-8
1979	Bishop Walsh High School	Boys	2-10
1980	Bishop Walsh High School	Boys	7-8
1981	Bishop Walsh High School	Boys	12-4
1982	Bishop Walsh High School	Boys	10-6
1983	Bishop Walsh High School	Boys	12-4-1
1984	Bishop Walsh High School	Boys	12-3-1

1985	Indiana University of Pennsylvania	Men	6-8-3
1986	Catonsville Community College	Women	0-8
1987	College of Notre Dame (Baltimore)	Women	3-3-2
1988	Montrose School	Boys	1-7
1990	Frostburg State University	Men	14-5-1
1992	Fort Hill High School	Boys	5-7
1993	Fort Hill High School	Boys	8-3-1
1994	Frostburg State University	Women	9-7-1
1995	Frostburg State University	Women	10-7-1
1996	Frostburg State University	Women	12-5-1
1997	Allegany High School	Boys	11-4-1
1998	Mt. Savage High School	Boys	13-3
1999	Mt. Savage High School	Boys	10-5
2000	Beall High School	Boys	14-1
2001	Beall High School	Boys	11-3-1
2006	Allegany College of Maryland	Men	7-6-3
2007	Allegany College of Maryland	Men	5-10-1
2008	Allegany High School	Boys	9-5-1
2009	Allegany High School	Boys	10-4-1
2010	Potomac State College	Men	8-6-1
2011	Potomac State College	Men	10-5-1
2012	Potomac State College	Men	16-3

2013	Potomac State College	Men	15-2-2
2014	Potomac State College	Men	11-8
2015	Potomac State College	Men	8-7
2016	Potomac State College	Men	5-9
2017	Bishop Walsh High School	Girls	3-12
2018	Bishop Walsh High School	Girls	11-8
2019	Bishop Walsh High School	Girls	12-3
2023	Lake Forest High School	Boys	4-10-1

Totals:

High School Record: 205-120-9

College Record: 139-88-16

Overall Record: 344-208-25

Athletic Directors I Have Worked For and With

Outstanding Leaders That I Always Appreciated!

Name	School / Organization
Brother Barry DiBartilo	Bishop Walsh High School
Sister Sharon Marie Slear	Bishop Walsh High School
Frank Cignetti	Indiana University of Pennsylvania
Joe Fusco	Westminster College
Betsy Alden	College of Notre Dame (Maryland)
Gary Keedy	Catonsville Community College

Loyal Park	Frostburg State University
Michael Calhoun	Fort Hill High School
Jack Gilmore	Allegany High School
Gene Paul	Mount Savage High School
Chris Kreiling	Beall High School
Bob Kirk	Allegany Community College
Duane McMinn	Allegany High School
Shawn White	Potomac State College
Carl Watson	Bishop Walsh School
Mike "Doc" Edwards	Bishop Walsh School
Fred Johnson	Lake Forest High School
Anthony Flores	Philadelphia Union – Technical Director
Phil Griffiths	Philadelphia Union – Technical Director

Coaches Who Worked With Me Over My 42 Years of Coaching Soccer

It Takes A Village! Thank You!

• Dr. Raul Felipa	• Ross Kiddy
• Dr. Diovanni Mastrangelo	• Connor Eberly
• Al Via	• Caleb Gooding

- Bill Garlitz
- Tim Rowan
- Joe Rowan
- Mike Nolan
- Vince Celtnieks
- Jay Hegeman
- Carl Reese
- Steve Clark
- Brad Burr
- Ron Plourde
- Alan Green
- Darcy Legoy
- Joe Enright
- Dave Blank
- George Bishields
- Harry Youngblood
- Darrell Blank
- Rick Zimmerman
- Jeff Ruark
- Steve Amman
- Tom Dawson

- Donnie Amman
- Mark Sprouse
- Zach Hearn
- Mike Starkey
- Slug Armstrong
- Bob Harden
- Jodie Pebble
- Buck Smith
- Lisa Burkey
- John Meyer
- Kendall Miller
- Sister Sharon Marie Slear
- Sharon Lancaster
- Pat Nolan
- Dave Hobel
- Avalon LeDong

Letter from Erin Langan

Dear Dr. Kiddy,

I just wanted to thank you for everything you've done for me throughout high school. You have consistently supported me, and you've gone above and beyond the duties of a principal or coach to help me. You were understanding, no matter what the issue I presented to you. I am so thankful that I got to be a player on your soccer team. I always wanted to have you as a coach. I knew you could take us to the next level, and you did!

Thank you for everything you've done for me. I'll be forever grateful.

Sincerely,

Erin Langan

Bishop Walsh School   Class of 2019

P.S. Thanks for (Kinda) carrying me off the field when I sprained my ankle.

Letter from Tim Travis

March 12, 2019

Dear Ray,

Just a few years ago, I came to the sad conclusion that my school, my children's school, and my grandchildren's school would probably not exist for long, especially with the new Allegany High School coming. Little did I know that someone was watching out for us!

I don't know how it all began, but whatever buttons you pushed, bells you rang, or calls you made, you rescued our school from the edge of ashes.

I cannot write well enough to express to you the difference you've made at Bishop Walsh.

I walked in the building, at your invitation, and I saw heads up, smiles on faces, and a buzz in the hallways, and positive attitudes throughout. You took a tremendous challenge in this situation, and month by month, call by call, meeting by meeting, game by game, you have changed the culture in and out of Bishop Walsh.

I have to tell you as that clock winds down on Friday's game with Mt. St. Joe's, tears filled my eyes. We had never won a game on the second night ever!

I told you before, I have gone to sleep smiling every night since September.

You were the perfect guy to create all of this positive energy. I believe there is more to come. Keep up the great work.

Thank you!

Miles Of Smiles

Tim Travis, Bishop Walsh Alum 1969

Letter From Matt Zealand

Dear Coach Kiddy,

I just wanted to take the time during the Christmas holiday to wish you a Merry Christmas and thank you for a wonderful season. With this being my senior year, I really wanted things to go well, especially after the extremely disappointing preceding year. When Andy and I heard we had a new coach, we were ecstatic. We soon learned our hopes were justified.

Any man who could bring together the rather rowdy group of us and bring us back from the rocky beginning we had to 11-4-1 deserves high praise. You are truly an excellent coach who I feel has a particularly outstanding way of communication with your players. I have been on a lot of talented teams with some knowledgeable coaches; but quite often a lack of communication brings the team down. Such was not the case this year.

I also really appreciate the faith you had, not only in our team as a whole, but in me individually. You stuck with me even when I was having a rough time of it and continued to give me a chance to prove myself. I couldn't have asked for anything more. I only wish we could've won the Region. But there is no use crying over missed penalty shots now-we truly had a great year.

Just to let you know, the same thing hasn't happened (yet) in basketball that happened in soccer-you know having a great start is important-I've been laid up now for two and half weeks, with a badly sprained left ankle. But as you know these things happen and I'll be back... I just hope we can put together the same kind of season that we had in soccer.

Once again, I would just like to thank you and wish you and your family the best. I expect Allegany soccer to do well next season-no excuses, you better take it to Flintsone (and for Pete's sake, you better beat Walsh). So good Luck and Merry Christmas. I'll see you around.

Sincerely,

Matt Zealand

Allegany H.S. Class of 1998

www.ingramcontent.com/pod-product-compliance
Lightning Source LLC
Chambersburg PA
CBHW071714120626

46550CB00001B/223